Wendy W

Puppy training with love and respect: A modern approach to puppy training essentials

Copyright 2020 by SP Market Connection LLC – All rights reserved.

All rights Reserved. No part of this publication or the information in it may be quoted from or reproduced in any form by means such as printing, scanning, photocopying, or otherwise without prior written permission of the copyright holder.

Disclaimer and Terms of Use: Effort has been made to ensure that the information in this book is accurate and complete; however, the Author and the Publisher do not warrant the accuracy of the information, text, and graphics contained within the book due to the rapidly changing nature of science, research, known and unknown facts, and internet. The Author and the publisher do not hold any responsibility for errors, omissions, or contrary interpretation of the subject matter herein. This book is presented solely for motivational and informational purposes only.

―――――――――――

Hi there,

If you're reading this, you must be on your way to getting a companion of a thousand adventures. An intelligent and obedient dog to have a real bond with.

To support you on this journey, I've got a gift for you – your own training calendar where you'll be able to keep a record of your pup's progress.

Please scan the QR code below to download a free printable copy.

I hope the training will be beneficial for both you and your dog.

Cheers,
Wendy

Table of Contents

Introduction 7
    Three essential things you need to know before you bring your puppy home......................7
    So, Before You Get Started..9
    Frequently Asked Questions 10

Potty Training 13
    Getting Organized 13
    Puppy Pads 15
    Getting into a Routine 20
    Adding in Your Cue 22
    Key Tips for Success..23
    But What About When You Can't Supervise?.....................................26
    When Mistakes Happen..27
    Medical Issues Which Can Affect Potty Training...................................31

Crate Training 34
    Benefits of Crate Training...35

Choosing the Right Crate for Your Puppy 39

The 6 Step Process to Crate Training 42

Reminders for Successful Crate Training 51

Why Train Your Puppy? 54

Reinforcements 56

Training for Life 57

Consistency 58

Criteria 59

Thinking About Cues 61

Generalizing a Behavior – Any Time, Any Place, Anywhere! 62

Techniques 64

Lure and Reward 64

Clicker Training 65

Target Training 67

Training the Behaviors 71

"Sit" 71

"Down" 75

Tips for Teaching a "Down" to a Small Dog 81

Recall 82

Puppy Recall Game 87

"Stay" 89

"Leave It" 94

Trouble Shooting 98

Training Your Puppy to Walk on a Loose Leash 101

Getting Organized for Training Loose Leash Walking 101

Leash Training 104

Introducing the Leash 109

Ongoing Loose Leash Training 111

Managing Pulling and Distractions 112

Behavioral Issues and How to Resolve Them 115

Training a rescue dog 116

Aggression 120

Food Related Aggression 123

Barking 125

Chewing 130

Adult Dogs Chewing 133

Jumping up 133

How to Stop Biting 139

Puppy Biting 139

Final words 143

Introduction

Three essential things you need to know before you bring your puppy home...

We know that you want straight-talking, right-at-it puppy training advice, so that's what we've aimed to provide. No fluff, no filler, just modern science-based, effective techniques.

There are three themes which you'll see throughout the book:

1. **Respect**

    The world of dog training has changed. No longer do you need to "dominate" or be a "pack leader" for your dog to be an obedient and loyal companion. We simply need to respect our pups in the same way that we show respect for each other. We know that dogs experience emotions in much the same way as we do, and we know that they can read our emotions from our facial expressions[1].

---
[1] https://www.sciencedaily.com/releases/2018/06/180620125955.htm

2. **Consistency**

Imagine living in a world where you didn't understand the language and where the priorities and ways of behaving were very different from your own. That must be an incredibly difficult situation to be in, yet it's what our pups face when they leave Mum and their littermates. Then imagine that the rules kept changing, what was allowed one day isn't the next. What was a definite "no" yesterday with one person is now a "yes" with a different person. The more consistent we can be, the quicker your pup will understand what's needed, and the less stressful it will be for everyone.

3. **Patience**

We all have bad days when we are not our usual friendly selves or don't much feel like socializing. Your pup is going to have those days as well. Give them a break, have a chill-out day and curl up on the sofa and watch a film. This is great bonding time!

When you apply each of these three themes to every one of your interactions with your pup, you're on your way to an amazing lifelong relationship.

So, Before You Get Started...

🐾 **Puppy training is simple but not always easy.**

That might sound a little confusing, but the basic concepts of training a puppy are simple. We reward the behaviors we want more of and ignore the behaviors we want less of. But the process of working with another living creature with their own wants and desires doesn't always make training an easy process. However, we've provided you with a complete tool kit to give you a head start on the skills and knowledge you need to train like a pro!

🐾 **Training is a mechanical skill.**

Or so top animal trainer Bob Bailey[2] tells us. What Bob means is that the more practice and planning you put into your training, the more effective the process will be. It may feel a little awkward to begin with to coordinate the leash and treats while spotting the exact moment your pup offers you the right behavior. But like any skill, the more you practice, the easier it becomes.

---

[2] https://stalecheerios.com/teaching-people/bob-bailey-teaching-trainers/

🐾 **Start training from day one.**

When training was all about forcing dogs into doing what we wanted them to do, the pup needed to be at least six months old to be able to cope with the physical nature of the process. Now that we know we can get great results without using any force, we can begin training as soon as our pup gets home.

🐾 **Slow and steady wins the day.**

The foundations you build when training your puppy will be with them throughout their life. Spend time developing your puppy's knowledge of each behavior you train. Make sure they offer it quickly and confidently before even thinking about pushing on to the next step.

Frequently Asked Questions

My pup sits perfectly in the home but won't do it on a walk. Why not?

Pups are pretty awful at what's called generalization, and that's the ability to be able to offer a learned behavior in a range of different environments. But the good news is that they get better at this with practice. Take a look at "Why Train Your Puppy?" for more information on teaching your pup how to generalize their behaviors.

My pup went outside to potty and then came back in and weed on the carpet. Why did they do that?

The outside world is so exciting for your puppy. So many smells and things to see and chew that sometimes they just forget what they went outside to do until they're back inside! Popping pup onto a leash can help to avoid fun and games and instead encourage them to focus on the task at hand. Our chapter on potty training provides more tips on making it easier for your pup to go in the right place, every time.

Those puppy teeth are so sharp! How do I stop my pup biting me?

Pups are a bit like babies in that they investigate everything by putting it into their mouths; the only problem is that pups have those razor-sharp teeth! Have a look at two games designed to help with this problem, "To get the treat you need to leave the treat alone," and "Swops," which you'll find in the Biting section of the Behavior Issues chapter.

Isn't a crate just a cage? Do I really need to use one?

There are very few absolutes in dog training. If you're able to always supervise your puppy, or you have somewhere they can safely be when you can't supervise them, then you may find that you don't need to worry about crate training. There are, though, lots of other benefits to teaching your puppy to be relaxed in a crate, and these are all included in our chapter on crate training.

As soon as I put a leash on my puppy, they start to pull. Now what?

Unclip the leash and head straight over to over to the section on leash-training. We recommend teaching your pup the right place to be before a leash is even put on. We also know that not all puppies learn in the same way, so we've included a couple of different techniques for you to try.

I keep hearing about clicker training. Can that be used with a puppy?

It sure can! And we provide details about the technique and step-by-step instructions on how to use it to teach new behaviors in the Training Your Puppy chapter.

Potty Training

If you've never celebrated with a puppy who has just had a wee, in the yard while it's pouring down rain, then get prepared! Part of having a puppy join the home is helping them to understand what it takes to be a great family member, and that includes the rules around where and when to relieve themselves.

Getting Organized

So, before you collect your puppy, there's some planning to do around the whole subject of potty training.

First off, where is the "Potty Zone" going to be? Some owners fence off a small section of the yard to keep toileting and child play areas separate. This also has the advantage of creating just one area which needs to be cleaned on a regular basis rather than the whole yard. If you don't have a yard, then you need to consider an area where your pup can go and not cause any problems for neighbors or children out playing.

Then think about what word or "cue" you're going to use to tell your puppy they need to empty themselves. This is such a useful thing for your pup to know. If they're going in the car or you're heading out without them, being able to ask them to "hurry up" means that they're much more likely to be accident-free.

The next thing to consider is where your pup will sleep so that you can avoid any night time accidents. We recommend using a crate, and so this guide includes a dedicated chapter to help you successfully crate train your puppy.

Finally, the food you decide to feed your pup will affect the potty-training process. High-quality food will mean fewer bowel movements each day. That's because the low-quality foods are often full of cheap fillers which have little nutritional value and are hard to digest. This means that it passes right through, resulting in more waste.

> 1,000 British pet owners, 50% men and 50% women, were asked if they preferred to snuggle with their pet or their partner:
> 54% of women preferred cuddles from their pet.
> 38% of men said they would prefer a pet cuddle.
> 10% of pet owners admitted that they secretly loved their pet more than their partners!

High-quality food tends to have ingredients that are high in nutritional value and are easily digested. So, more gets absorbed, and less passes out. You'll also find that your puppy's poo is firmer with good quality food. Not only does that make it easier to clean up after them, but it also helps your puppy to learn bowel control, and it reduces anal gland problems[3].

---

3   http://www.millenniumvets.co.uk/advice.aspx?a=1799&clientId=20107

Puppy Pads

There are several good reasons why you might decide to use puppy pads in the home rather than taking your pup outside. It could be that there's a delay before you can get your pup outside. Maybe you have to walk down several flights of stairs or wait for an elevator. It could also be that you have some mobility issues, meaning that it takes a little bit longer to reach the outside world. In these situations, you may find that your pup gets caught short halfway through the journey to get outside, resulting in the need for a clean-up job.

If you don't have access to your own outdoor space, then you'll need to keep your pup safe until they have completed their vaccinations. That will mean avoiding areas where other dogs have been. In this situation, puppy pads can be a great option.

Made with an absorbent top layer with plastic backing to prevent any leakage, puppy pads usually have some kind of attractant smell to them to encourage your pup to investigate and then relieve themselves. So, while they're more expensive than buying your local newspaper every day to cover the floor, they are much easier to use around the home.

Using Puppy Pads

1. Decide where in the house you'd like your pup to relieve themselves and place the pads down on the floor.

2. Place them somewhere you can keep an eye on, that way you can praise and reward your puppy when they go in the right place.

3. Ready to move from pads to outside? Just take a pad along with you and place it down on the ground. The attractant smell will be just the same as it was inside and so will encourage your pup to go potty.

4. If your pup is still not keen to go outside without the pad, slowly reduce the size of the pad, making it smaller and smaller until they're just using the ground.

Cons of Puppy Pads

While puppy pads can be really helpful in the potty-training process, there are some downsides you should be aware of when deciding whether to use them:

- They can be pretty confusing for the pup. Think about the logic for a moment; they get praised for toileting in the house. Anything we praise a dog for is likely to increase the likelihood of them doing it again. Do you really want to teach your pup that they get praised for relieving themselves inside your house?

While they may not look too tasty, some pups find them irresistible in the same way they love socks, shoes, and TV remote controls.

 Is that a puppy pad or is it a mat? While the attractant may help, your pup might just think that a soft texture under paw is the place to go. This is more likely to happen when you have a tiled or wooden floor with rugs.

 There is the potential to miss out on opportunities for socialization and fresh air. The outside world can be very distracting for our youngster. However, the more opportunities they have to experience all the noises and smells, the quicker they will become used to them and be less distracted.

Let's Start at the Very Beginning

You get home after picking up your puppy. The very first thing you're going to do is take them into the yard and let them empty themselves. This is all about setting your pup up for success. That very first toilet outside now sets the scene for the rest of the potty-training process. It also means that the scent from their urine is in the

Despite their name, Labrador Retrievers did not originate from Labrador. They actually came from the Newfoundland area of Canada. Formerly known as the St. John's Water Dog, they helped fishermen to retrieve fish and pull in the nets.

Their amazing working ability and friendly nature soon caught the eye of visitors from overseas. So, it wasn't long before they were traveling across the Atlantic to Scotland where they were developed into the Labrador we love and adore today.

right place. Dogs, with their amazing scenting abilities, "see" the world through their noses and are attracted back to the spot where they last went[4]. So, we definitely want that to be outside and not in the middle of the living room carpet!

Let Potty Training Begin

So, you've had your first success. Now, you can really focus on getting potty training started properly.

Potty training is all about getting into a routine. It's also about realizing your puppy's physical limitations. Until they are 16 weeks of age, your puppy doesn't have full control of their bladder. As for night time, the general rule is they'll need to go out after their age in months plus one hour. So, a four-month-old puppy will need the opportunity to go out after five hours of sleep, even during the night.

Now those are very broad guidelines. Some pups will be fully house trained and clean through the night by the time they're four months. Others may be much older. Small dogs can take longer to successfully house train, and that's thought to be because of their small bladder and fast metabolism[5]. If you keep your expectations to your dog being fully house-trained by the time they are six months old, then you've got a realistic goal to aim towards.

---

4   https://www.ncbi.nlm.nih.gov/pmc/articles/PMC6116041/

5   https://www.psychologytoday.com/us/blog/canine-corner/201909/is-house-training-more-effective-large-or-small-dogs

Playtime or Wee Time?

Hopefully, your pup will quickly decide that you're a great person to be around. Not only do you provide food, but you're also the source of fun and games. But, when you're outside, how does your pup know if it's playtime or potty time? A puppy who is leaping around and grabbing hold of your shoelaces is not what you need when you need to go out or get back to work.

So now, you need to be boring. With your pup on a leash, slowly walk up and down the yard with little interaction. Moving will stimulate your pup's bladder and bowels, making it more likely they will go potty. The leash is important firstly so that you'll know for sure when and where they have been if you need to clean up, and secondly, because it will prevent games in the yard as they run around and have fun.

Toilet breaks in the middle of the night, especially, should be boring; you don't want your pup to think making a noise in the crate means getting let out and having a great time.

Getting into a Routine

There will be certain times of the day when you can be pretty sure that your pup will need to able to relieve themselves. These include:

1. **First Thing in the Morning**

The moment your alarm clock goes off, your puppy is going to wake up. No longer is your first task of the day to brush your teeth or put the coffee on. Now it's to take your puppy straight outside.

If your puppy is sleeping in a crate, consider having it near your bed or very close to the bedroom. Then if you're awoken with the sound of your puppy whimpering, you'll know they need to go out. Pop the leash on and, if they're small enough, carry them outside to avoid an accident along the way.

10,000 pet owners in 11 different countries, were surveyed to find out which one treated their dogs most like family. The US came out as being the most lenient with house rules!

90% of US pet owners say the top benefit of owning a pet is that it makes them happy.

48% of US dogs are given free access to get onto furniture compared to 15% in France.

41% of US dogs are likely to sleep in their owner's bed, but only 14% get to cuddle up in Spain.

2. **After Meals**

Around 5 to 30 minutes after eating, your pup will need to go to the toilet. So, keeping meal times to a good routine makes it easier for your puppy to also get into a toileting schedule. While you may decide to free feed your adult dog by leaving food down all the time, that is going to create havoc with the house-training process. A puppy who chooses to have a big meal just before bedtime is going to need to go out several times in the night.

If, however, you feed at set times, then you'll know when to take your puppy outside. The younger the puppy, the quicker they will need to go once they have a full stomach.

Young pups will be eating three to four meals a day, and most will need to poop after each meal, so don't get distracted during these key times. This also means that you can schedule their meal times to make sure that there is plenty of time to toilet before bedtime.

If your pup has just had a long drink, then that's also going to be a cue to provide them with time outside.

3. After Playtime and Anything Exciting!

Running around means that your pup's digestive tract is stimulated, which in turn means that they may need a potty break. Keep an eye out for them suddenly stopping the game and beginning to sniff. If they've had a "zoomie" session, running around like a thing possessed, then you can be sure that it's going to be followed by the need to relieve themselves.

Exciting things might be a visitor arriving or playing with another dog. In the excitement, they may forget about needing to go out until it's too late. Help your pup to get it right by letting them go outside as soon as they have got over the initial excitement.

4. **After a Nap**

Waking up after a nap is just like the early morning routine. So, arrange the room so that their bed or crate is close by to where you'll be. That way, you can immediately scoop them up and take them outside as soon as they wake up.

Adding in Your Cue

We mentioned right at the very start of this section, the big advantage of having a dog who will toilet on cue. This might be something like "hurry up" or "go toilet." To teach your puppy what this means, just quietly and calmly say your cue while your pup is relieving themselves. They won't immediately know what those words mean, but over time, they'll make the connection, especially if the result is rewarded with their favorite treat or a game.

In fact, world-renowned dog trainer, Ian Dunbar makes a great analogy. He says, "Once your pup realizes that her eliminatory products are the equivalent of coins in a food vending machine — that feces and urine may be cashed in for tasty treats —

your pup will be clamoring to eliminate in the appropriate spot because soiling the house does not bring equivalent fringe benefits."

As tempting as it can be to get excited when they do finally go, there's a pretty good chance they'll stop mid-flow to join in the celebration. So, quiet and calm is the way to go here.

Did you know that there's a connection between obedience training and your dog becoming house trained?[6] Researchers found that dogs who had undertaken training were much more likely to be clean in the house than those that hadn't. Check out our chapter on teaching your puppy the basic commands for tips and advice.

Key Tips for Success

1. **Set Alarms**

It won't be long before you know your pup's schedule, and you'll be able to spot those tell-tale signs that they need to get outside quickly. But when we get

> During World War I and II, Allied countries aimed to eliminate or change anything with the word "German" in its name. So that meant that the "German Shepherd dog" (GSD) simply became the "Shepherd Dog," In the UK, they became the "Alsatian" after the Alsace area on the French/German border. In the 1970s, they once again became known as the German Shepherd Dog.

---

6   https://www.sciencedirect.com/science/article/pii/S1558787819300991

involved in something else, it can be really easy to miss things, and before you know it there's a puddle to clean up on the floor.

So, set alarms on your mobile phone for every 2 hours during the day. That way, even if you are deeply engrossed in work, playing with the kids, or reading a good book, you'll get that reminder to check in on your pup's needs.

2. **Keep an Umbrella by the Door**

In the early stages of potty training, you're going to be spending quite a bit of time outside waiting for your pup to go. When it's raining outside, many puppies decide that it's far too wet to go outside and that kitchen rug looks look a much more comfortable option! That means that you'll need to go out with your pup whatever the weather is. Having an umbrella by the door ready to grab in wet weather makes it much more attractive to head outside.

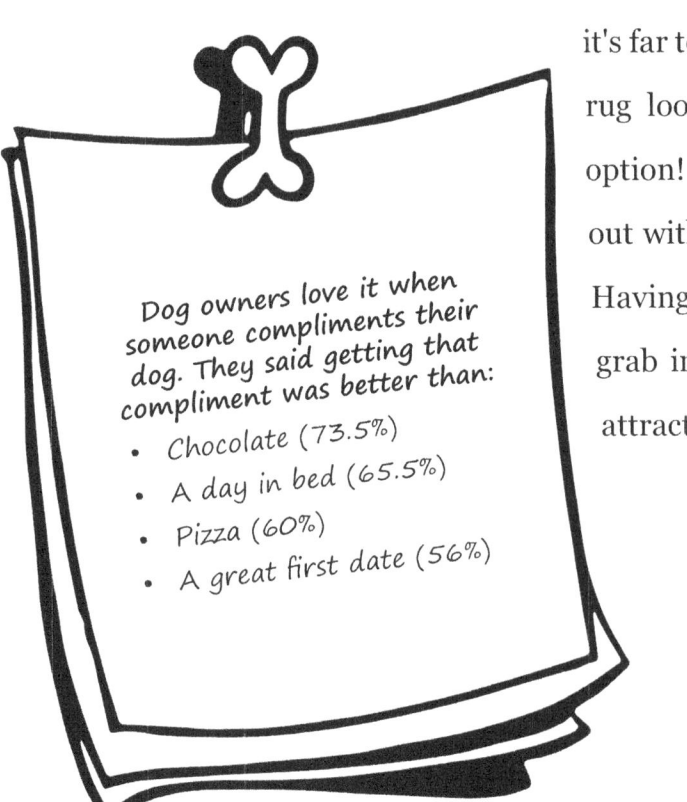

Dog owners love it when someone compliments their dog. They said getting that compliment was better than:
- Chocolate (73.5%)
- A day in bed (65.5%)
- Pizza (60%)
- A great first date (56%)

3. **Keep Treats on Hand**

Along with your umbrella, but kept out of reach from your pup, keep some treats in a tub with a lid. That means that you're all ready to praise and reward every single time they perform outside.

4. **Don't Be in a Hurry**

Be careful, and don't be in a hurry, especially in bad weather. Your pup can quickly learn how to bob down as if they were relieving themselves and then run up to you for their treat before you both rush back to the inside warmth. Five minutes later, you spot a puddle on the floor. If you've been going out with your puppy for a while, you'll know how long it takes and, believe it or not, what a "fake" looks like, too. Don't kid yourself it'll be fine. Your pup has now learned how to get back into the home super quick, and meanwhile, you're on your knees cleaning up.

5. **Door Open, Door Closed?**

If the door to reach the yard is always open, then your pup doesn't learn how to ask to go outside. Now that might be fine during the summer, but when you have the door closed during the colder months, you may find that's some missing knowledge. Another downside of the door always being open is that you may not know if your pup has toileted, especially important when it comes to settling them down for bed at night time.

But What About When You Can't Supervise?

Maybe you're going out somewhere that your pup can't go, it's going to mean that you're not there to supervise trips out to the yard. So, first things first, think about routines for meals. If you know that pup needs to go out 10 minutes after eating, then get that part of the day done before you go out. A sleepy puppy is less likely to need to go to the toilet, so have a good game, provide the opportunity to go out, and then they might just nap their way through your departure. Just make sure you're back before they wake up!

This might be a time when crate training would be really helpful. Generally, pups don't like to mess in their sleeping area, so a crate can help a youngster hold on until you get home. Don't forget, though, that they physically can't hold on until around 16 weeks of age, and the last thing you want to do is place your puppy in a situation where they do soil their bedding. That's not a habit you want to encourage. And as discussed by The Humane Society of the United States[7], a crate is not a magical solution; when it's not used correctly, a dog can feel trapped and frustrated.

The quickest way to crack potty training is to set things up so that your pup can go in the right place every time. So, if you know you can't be there to supervise your youngster, you might want to call on the help of friends or family, or hire a dog walker to pop in and spend time with your puppy.

---

7   https://www.humanesociety.org/resources/crate-training-101

When Mistakes Happen

With the best will in the world, there will be mistakes. You take your eye off them for a moment, and when you turn around, they've woken up and left you a little "present." Then you get a newspaper, roll it up and whack yourself over the head, chanting "I will get better at supervising my puppy!"

In all seriousness, the last thing you want to happen is for your pup to connect going to the toilet with you getting mad at them. They might make the connection of toileting inside = punishment, but they might also assume that it's toileting = punishment. When that happens, your pup then is reluctant to go in front of you; now, you have a whole heap of other problems to sort out. These guys are so good at picking up our emotions. Did you know, for example, that dogs can actually smell how happy we are?[8] So that means we really need to think about how we react and how that's going to affect the relationship we have with them. And if you think about it,

Golden Retrievers have been a favorite breed for two US presidents.

Ronald Reagan's favorite dog was Victory, a Golden Retriever. Victory lived on Regan's Californian ranch along with two Scottish Terriers called Scotch and Soda, and a Bouvier des Flandres called Lucky.

But Reagan was not the only president to be charmed by the Golden Retriever. President Ford had two Goldens, called Liberty and Misty, along with a Siamese cat and a mixed-breed dog.

---

8   https://www.researchgate.net/publication/320265642_Interspecies_transmission_of_emotional_information_via_chemosignals_from_humans_to_dogs_Canis_lupus_familiaris

the mistakes that do happen are usually our fault. No punishment means no angry face, no shouting or angry words, and definitely no rubbing their nose in it.

It can be tough to keep calm when you've been trying your best and just turn your back for a second only to come back and see that steaming pile of poo on your carpet. That's the time to take your pup to another room, or outside if it's safe for them to be by themselves for a few minutes. With them out of the way, you can calm down, clear your frustration, and then get on with cleaning up.

It's essential to get rid of all the odor to make sure that your pup isn't tempted to go right back to that spot next time they need to go. First off, remove the bulk of the mess. So that means using a dry absorbent cloth or paper towels to soak up urine and either a poo bag or paper towels to pick up the poop.

Next, you need to get rid of all that odor. Urine is composed of three elements. The first two, sticky urea and urochrome, can be washed away. However, the third, which is uric acid, is pretty much impossible to dissolve and remove from surfaces using water. That means you need a product specially designed for the job.

Many household cleaning products have ammonia in them, just the same as in your puppy's urine. That then means that the product may cause the area to become really attractive as the potty spot. So, instead, you need to get a good enzymatic or bio-based neutralizing product from the pet store. These solutions often act as a cleaner as well – meaning that you can clean and deodorize in one step.

Building a History of Success

Every time your puppy relieves themselves outside, it's like putting a coin in a piggy bank. You're building up a history of success. When there's an accident inside, then one of those coins is taken back out. Your puppy's potty training can survive a few withdrawals. Mistakes will happen. However, if you become overdrawn, then that's the time to take a moment to work out what needs to change to get back in credit.

Excitement Urination

When it's really exciting for your puppy, such as when you come home or visitors arrive, you may fund that your puppy dribbles or squirts small amounts of urine. This isn't uncommon in young dogs, and most grow out of the behavior as they leave puppyhood behind.

The easiest way to manage this is to do all greetings outside where a little bit of wee won't matter. Do remember, though, that your pup probably hasn't emptied their bladder when this happens. So, after the initial excitement has subsided, then do encourage them to go toilet.

You can also try keeping calm, so downplaying greetings until they have relieved themselves, and then you can say your hellos. It's essential not to punish your puppy for excitement urination; they have no control over it, so telling them off will not stop it happening. What it will do is to start breaking down the relationship you have with your youngster.

Submissive Urination

In trying to communicate that they are no threat, some pups will roll over on to their backs and urinate. This usually happens when people reach toward the puppy to say hello or if you're telling your puppy off.

Submissive urination is also most common in younger dogs, and many will outgrow the behavior if you manage the situation correctly when they're a pup. So that means appearing less threatening when approaching your puppy by kneeling down and then let them come to you when they're ready. Avert your gaze so that you're not staring right at them and then gently stroke under the chin or on their chest.

Did you know that every year an average dog owner in the UK will:
- Walk more than 1,000 miles exercising their pet.
- Play 2,080 rounds of fetch.
- Call their pet's name 3,120 times while walking them.

Again, punishment by physically scolding your pup or using a stern voice will make the problem worse. Your puppy is trying hard to tell you that they're feeling a little worried and anxious; telling them off will just reduce their confidence even further. If you don't feel that you're making progress with what seems to be submissive urination, do talk to your vet as it is often confused with incontinence issues[9].

Medical Issues Which Can Affect Potty Training

What if you're following all the guidance, and you're being extra vigilant watching your pup, but there are still more accidents inside than there are outside? This is the time to get in touch with your veterinarian because some medical conditions can make it tough for your pup to be successfully potty trained.

Bladder Infections

If bacteria make its way into your pup's bladder, then it can cause an infection. These can create a whole range of symptoms[10], including loss of house training and needing to toilet more often. Your vet will probably ask for a urine sample, which lets them work out which bacteria are causing the problem. A course of antibiotics is then usually prescribed to get it all cleared up.

---

9   https://www.vetmed.wsu.edu/outreach/Pet-Health-Topics/categories/common-problems/urinary-incontinence

10   https://www.ovrs.com/blog/when-you-gotta-go-urinary-tract-infection-in-dogs/

Ectopic Ureter

Your pup can be born with a defect called ectopic ureter, which causes incontinence. The ureters are responsible for carrying urine from the kidneys to the bladder, but it is possible for one or both of them to by-pass the bladder and connect somewhere else. As a result, your pup may drip urine. It's more common for female dogs to have this problem than males, and according to the College of Veterinary Medicine at Washington State University[11], there are seven breeds that also seem to have a higher occurrence of this problem. These include:

- Siberian Husky

- Labrador Retriever

- Collie

- Welsh Corgi

- Wire-Haired Fox Terrier

- West Highland White Terrier

---

[11] https://www.vetmed.wsu.edu/outreach/Pet-Health-Topics/categories/common-problems/urinary-incontinence

When there is a problem with just one ureter, then your pup will dribble urine, but they will also be able to urinate normally. If both ureters are affected, then they will only be able to dribble urine. Because of this, it can sometimes be misdiagnosed as simply a bladder infection. The warning signs are when everything seems to be improving while your pup is taking the antibiotics, but then the problem comes back again.

Surgery is usually needed so that the ureter can be moved to the correct place in the bladder, and then you'll be all set to get that potty training completed.

Crate Training

Imagine having somewhere that you can feel safe, where you can snuggle into a comfy bed and know that you're not going to be disturbed? Sounds wonderful, doesn't it? Then imagine that you're able to keep your puppy safe while you're out and not dread coming home to see what's been destroyed. That probably sounds pretty good, too. This is the reality of crate training when introduced carefully and used effectively.

You'll sometimes see a crate described as a den for your dog, and while dogs aren't technically "den dwelling animals," they do like the safety that comes from a secure den-like space.

You might also see a crate being compared to a "jail cell," but when used correctly they will become a place where your pup chooses to go when tired, and where you can ensure that they're not getting up to mischief when you're not around to supervise.

Benefits of Crate Training

Safety and Forming Good Habits

We've already mentioned being able to leave you puppy in safety while you pop out, and that's because many of us have homes where it is difficult to leave a young pup without there being some kind of danger for them. Whether it's electric cords or ornaments, not only is there the risk to the puppy but also the upset for you from any damage they cause. It would be like leaving a two-year-old child to roam the house by themselves and expecting there to be no problems!

The Paws Rescue Organization[12] makes an excellent point that it's not just about avoiding damage; it's also about

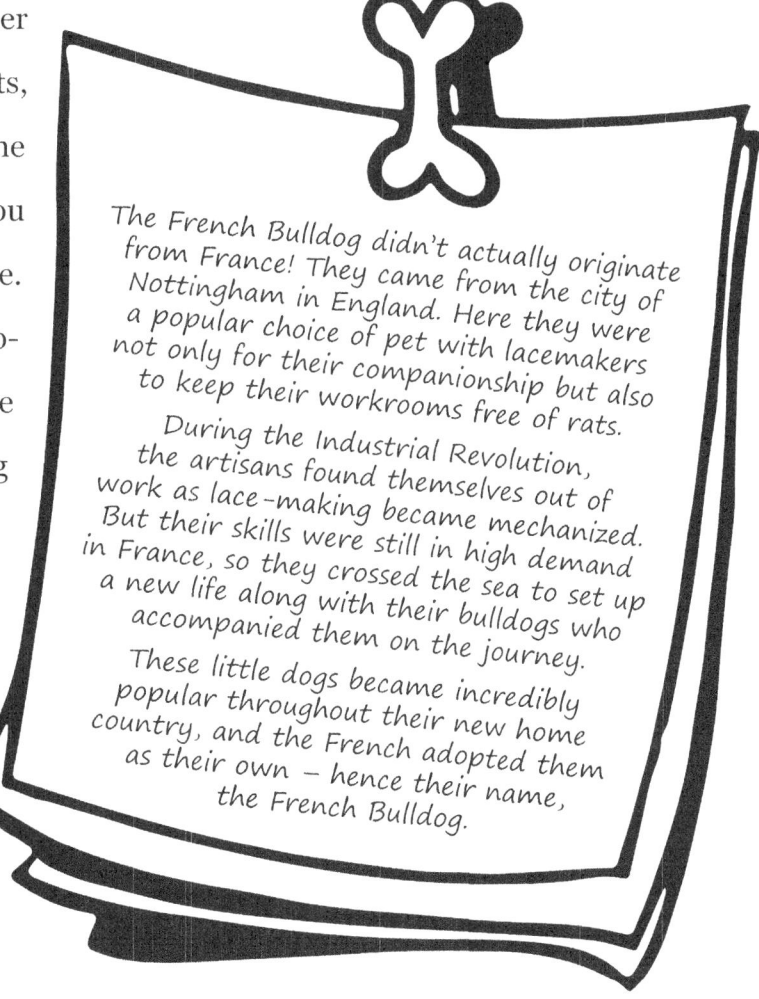

The French Bulldog didn't actually originate from France! They came from the city of Nottingham in England. Here they were a popular choice of pet with lacemakers not only for their companionship but also to keep their workrooms free of rats.

During the Industrial Revolution, the artisans found themselves out of work as lace-making became mechanized. But their skills were still in high demand in France, so they crossed the sea to set up a new life along with their bulldogs who accompanied them on the journey.

These little dogs became incredibly popular throughout their new home country, and the French adopted them as their own — hence their name, the French Bulldog.

---

12 https://www.paws.org/resources/the-benefits-of-crate-training/

preventing bad habits from even beginning. That means that if your puppy is never in the position where they can start chewing the table leg, then that's a problem you're never going to have to solve.

Place of Safety

When a crate is carefully introduced, it can become a place of safety that your dog can retreat to. This could be when something happens that startles them such as thunderstorms or fireworks. While the crate doesn't fix the problem, it does provide a refuge while you work on helping them to cope with the scary noises.

It might also be a chill out zone for your puppy if you have young children. Puppies and children can form amazing relationships, but there may be times when your four-legged youngster needs to escape to somewhere a little quieter. This also develops an excellent rule for your children, that when the puppy is in the crate, they're not to be disturbed. Family Paws Parent Education[13] also suggests that children never be allowed to get into the crate – your dog's cozy spot needs to be safe and kid-free!

Helps with Potty Training

Dogs generally like to keep their sleeping area clean; even very young puppies will move away from where they nap to relieve themselves. This means that when your pup

---

13   https://www.familypaws.com/kids-crates/

is in the crate, it will help them to develop control and be clean overnight. However, do remember that your pup does not have control over their toileting at first; it's something that they develop over a period of time. If you keep your pup in the crate too long and they toilet, they may lose that desire to keep their sleeping area clean.

Vet Visits

There may come an emergency where your pup needs to spend time at the veterinary office. It may also be that you're planning on your pup being neutered, so that will mean that they need to spend time in a crate, waiting for their operation time and then recovering from the anesthetic afterwards. If the first time that your pup ever goes in a crate is during a vet visit, then that's going to make an already stressful situation even tougher for them. If your puppy already knows how to relax in a crate, then that's going to be one less thing that they have to cope with.

Safe Car Transport

If your pup is safe and calm when in the car, you can focus on getting to your destination without becoming distracted. In a 2019 report[14], AAA found that one out of three owners admitted to being distracted by their dog when driving. When combined with research that shows that looking away from the road for just 2 seconds doubles your chance of being in a crash, it's essential that you don't become distracted.

---

14 https://news.aaa-calif.com/news/aaa-kurgo-pet-traffic-safety-survey-167646?zip=90019&devicecd=PC&referer=news.aaa-calif.com

Using a secured crate in the car can be the perfect way for your pup to travel in safety.

Safe Place When Visitors Arrive

When a pup joins your home, you can be sure that you'll get lots of visitors! Now, some may be really dog-savvy, and they'll follow your instructions on how to interact with your pup. The last thing you want is someone who encourages them to jump up because that's all your hard work on polite greetings down the drain! It may also be that you have visitors, such as young children who are a little nervous about meeting your new arrival, especially as pups can nibble on fingers.

Only 40% of dogs get to run off-leash on a walk, and that's because:
- 31% of owners are worried about other dogs.
- 31% of owners feel it's too dangerous.
- 18% of dogs aren't well behaved off the leash.
- 17% aren't allowed to be off-leash in the area they walk.

This is another time when having a crate trained puppy can remove all the stress from the situation. And once the initial excitement is over and your pup has calmed down, then that can be a good time to make new friends.

Getting Comfortable with Their Own Company

As tempting as it might be to have your pup follow you around everywhere, it does just make it tougher for them when you have to leave them on their own. Even if you sit beside the crate to begin with, it still creates a distance that you can slowly increase until they're settled, while you get on with jobs around the house. This is so useful when you're doing DIY jobs such as painting that get a little tricky with your pup "helping!"

Provides a Home away from Home

The Association of Professional Dog Trainers[15] makes a great point about the value of crates when traveling. Even if the room might be different, the crate is just the same as at home. That means that your puppy will know how to settle down and sleep at night, no matter where they are.

Choosing the Right Crate for Your Puppy

Now, you may be thinking a crate is a crate, but there are actually a few different types to choose from. So, let's look at those first, and then we'll move on to thinking about sizing.

Wire Mesh Crates are probably the ones you're most familiar with. They usually fold flat, making it easy to get them home and store if you no longer need them in the

---

[15] https://apdt.com/about/position-statements/

home. In the base of the crate, you should find a plastic tray so that your pup doesn't need to stand on the mesh. Now those trays do tend to be quite slippery, so you will need plenty of bedding so that your pup can safely sit and stand up without sliding all over the place. The ease with which the door opens varies from model to model, so do check this out in the store. If you can pull on the door a few times and it opens, it's not going to take long for your puppy to learn how to do that too!

Fabric Crates do away with the "cage" look, but they are usually only suitable for older dogs. That's because they won't stand up to chewing from those sharp little puppy teeth. Another reason why they may not be puppy proof is that they fasten up with a zip, and it's not going to take long for a smart puppy to work out how to open that up! Fabric crates are also very lightweight, which means that if they're not secured down, it's easy for your pup to move them around as if they were on a hamster wheel!

Keeping everything fresh and clean can be a problem with fabric crates. An accident on the plastic tray of the wire cage is easy to clean and disinfect; a wee on the floor of the fabric crate is going to soak through to your carpet.

Travel or Airline Crates are made of tough plastic designed to withstand being transported around the world. Although more expensive, these will last a long time so they could be a good buy if you're considering long-term use. Because they have solid sides, they are quite dark, which can mean that some dogs can be reluctant to go into them, and that plastic might prove irresistible to a teething puppy.

What Size of Crate for Your Puppy?

Size is an important consideration when shopping for a crate. Your pup needs to be able to sit up straight and turn around when inside. They also need to be able to stretch out and go to sleep comfortably. If your puppy is going to be a large breed, you may want to buy a crate with their adult size in mind. You can then block off some of the space to reduce the temptation for them to soil the crate.

Crates are generally sized according to the height and weight of the dog. If you're not sure of these for the grown-up version of your puppy, have a look at the AKC breed guides[16] for some guidance.

The Bulldog has been through several transformations to become the docile and loyal companions they are now well known for being.

The breed was originally created in the 13th century for the gruesome sport of bull-baiting, where a pack of fearless dogs would be released against a staked bull. The spectators would then bet on who would win, bull or dogs.

Thankfully in 1835, England banned blood sports, but illegal pit-dog fighting soon became popular. However, this needed a much quicker dog, and the Bulldog faced the reality of becoming extinct.

Luckily for the breed, their fans began the process of transforming these "fighters" into the perfect companion.

By 1886, breeders had altered the course for their beloved Bulldogs to develop a sweet dog who adores being around children.

---

16   https://www.akc.org/dog-breeds/

Where Should You Place Your Pup's Crate?

The aim is for the crate to be somewhere that your pup can relax and chill out. So that means that they need to be somewhere that's quiet and where they're not going to be constantly disturbed.

Also, think about temperature control, which will be especially important if your pup is one who may experience breathing problems such as a Pug or Boston Terrier. Avoid areas right next to a radiator, under an aircon unit, or which will be in direct sunlight.

Now, the crate will keep your pup safe from most dangers, but make sure there are no cables or plants which they might be able to nibble on right through the bars.

The 6 Step Process to Crate Training

So, you've read all about the benefits of crate training, and you've now decided that this is the right approach for your youngster. Your dog's love of his crate and his perception of it being a very positive place all comes down to the crate training process. We're going to guide you through six key steps in building that love which will last throughout their lifetime.

There's no set timescale for how long it will take, as it very much depends on your puppy's personality. Outgoing, confident pups may be running into their crate within a few days, whereas the more hesitant type may need a few weeks. Don't worry if you can't train every day. Scientists found that although dogs do learn when trained every day, the best results came from training once or twice a week[17].

Things You'll Need for Crate Training

1. The crate. No surprise for this to be number one on our list!

2. Comfy bedding. We want the crate to be somewhere your pup wants to go, so being warm and inviting makes it extra tempting.

3. Some treats. Very small ones are best because we just want your puppy to have a taste and want more rather than for them to become full quickly. Soft treats they can eat quickly are the best option.

4. Toys you can stuff with food or a long-lasting chew.

Step One - Introductions

Step one is all about building what's called a conditioned emotional response (CER). Kaiser Canine[18] describes the CER as "the feeling a dog has about a specific stimulus or

---

17 https://www.academia.edu/15202975/The_effect_of_frequency_and_duration_of_training_sessions_on_acquisition_and_long-term_memory_in_dogs

18 https://www.kaisercanine.com/blog/2016/1/8/the-conditioned-emotional-response

environment." At the start of crate training, your puppy has no real emotional response to the crate, or they may feel a little nervous about this new thing that's appeared in their home. Developing a positive CER means that your puppy will come to love their crate.

Now We Know How to Convert Dog Years to Human Years

If you asked an owner how old their dog is in human years, they would probably take their dog's age and multiply it by seven. So, a four-year-old dog would the equivalent of a 28-year-old person. However, researchers say that we have got that all wrong.

The seven-year logic came from taking a dog's lifespan of 10 years and a human lifespan of 70 years and simply dividing one by the other, so that seven human years equals one dog year. The research undertaken at UC San Diego School of Medicine and Moores Cancer Center, however, tells us that dogs age much more quickly than previously thought. This means that your one-year-old dog is much closer to 31 human years, and your five-year-old dog is equivalent to a 54-year-old human.

Dogs seem to enter middle age quite early, so we need to be careful with our dogs.

If our seven-year-old dog, who is already the equivalent of a 62-year-old human senior, wants to relax more than he used to, we should let him be.

1. To get ready, set up the crate with the door open and place it in the corner of the room. That way, your pup has a choice over whether they go near this new thing or not.

2. Then, throw a few treats on the floor outside of the crate. This will encourage your pup to investigate without any pressure to go inside.

3. Now place a few treats just inside the crate. Aim to position them so that puppy can lean in and reach them as they may not be ready to go all the way in yet.

4. Slowly aim the treats further and further into the crate until the puppy is going all the way in.

You're ready for step two when your puppy goes all the way into the crate without any hesitation.

Step Two – Meals in the Crate

To really develop that very positive CER, you're now going to feed your puppy their meals in the crate. Take the food-filled bowl and place it into the crate so that your pup needs to go all the way in to get their meal.

You're ready for step three when your puppy runs into their crate when they see you coming with their bowl.

Step Three – Close the Crate Door

1. With pup eating their meal, close the crate door and hold closed with your hand.

2. Just before your puppy has finished their food, open the door.

Just holding the door closed rather than bolting it, means that you can very quickly reopen it before your pup even thinks about crying to get back out.

You're ready for step 4 when your puppy pays no attention to the door closing.

Step Four – Adding the Cue

A cue is a word or action which tells your dog which behavior that you'd like them to complete. The cue for going into the crate might simply be the word "crate." Whatever the cue is, it should only mean one thing, in this case, go into your crate. You also need a second cue, and this one means "okay, now you can leave your crate." This second cue stops your puppy leaping up and trying to squeeze past before you've had the opportunity to fully open the gate. This cue might be "free" or "out."

Susan Garrett, a top dog agility handler and trainer, talks about the importance of not adding the cue too soon[19]. She suggests that you wait until you can predict that your

---

[19] https://susangarrettdogagility.com/2018/09/when-do-i-add-a-cue/

puppy will offer the behavior, and you love the way they are performing it. So, for our crate training, that means that your puppy happily and eagerly goes into their crate whenever you place their food bowl or treat inside.

1. Place a treat in the crate, and as your puppy enters, say your cue word for going in the crate. Once inside, give another treat and then say your release cue and encourage your pup to come out.

2. Repeat five times.

3. Now just wait a moment and see if your pup enters the crate by themselves if they do, then use your "in" cue as they enter and reward with a treat. Then as they leave, use your release cue. If your puppy doesn't enter the crate by themselves, simply return to and repeat step one.

4. Repetition is needed now so that your puppy can make the link between the cue, entering the crate and getting their treat.

You're ready to move to step five when your puppy goes into their crate when you give the cue.

Step Five – Adding Duration

So far, your pup has been coming in and out of the crate without spending too much time in there. This step is all about slowly building up the amount of time that your pup can be in the crate for.

While you're going through this stage, it's important to take into account the emotional state of your puppy. Are they calm and relaxed while in the crate, or are they pawing at the gate, anxious and whining? Having a great chew or food-filled toy to keep your pup busy will really build their desire to go in the crate and stay there.

Adding duration to a behavior requires a steady, step-by-step process. So, if your puppy is becoming distressed, then that's a signal for you that you need to backtrack in the plan. You need your puppy to be happy and calm when in their crate so that they can settle and then fall asleep. The stages in this step should be completed over several days rather than being crammed into a few training sessions.

Remember that the crate is all about calm behavior and chilling out, so you need to ensure that your training takes on the same style. Rather than opening the crate being a big celebration, keep everything low key so that your pup isn't desperate to get out and have a game with you. If they perceive that inside the crate is dull and outside is exciting, then you can be sure about where they would rather be!

1. Throw the chew stick or food-filled toy in the crate and give your "in" cue.

2. As your pup goes in, close the gate and count to three.

3. Open the gate and give your "out" cue encouraging your puppy to come out with a treat.

4. Retrieve the chew/toy, show it to your pup and throw it back in the crate.

5. Add one second to the time the gate is closed, repeating until you reach 10.

6. Now repeat adding five seconds to the time the gate is closed, so that's 10, 15, 20, etc.

7. When you reach one minute, then add ten seconds to the time the gate is closed, so that's 70, 80, 90, etc.

As scent hounds, Beagles love to follow a trail. They've got around 220 million scent receptors in their noses, compared to only 5 million in humans. So, it's no wonder that they're used by law enforcement to sniff out anything which shouldn't be there!

But that isn't the only way that amazing scent ability has been put to work. A Beagle called Elvis was trained to determine whether a polar bear was pregnant by smelling her poop! It seems that it can be incredibly hard to tell if a polar bear is really pregnant, but Elvis can spot samples from pregnant females, and he can do it with 97 percent accuracy!

8. Finally, when you reach 2 minutes, you can then increase the time by 1-minute increments.

Puppies are hugely individual when it comes to learning these types of behaviors. Some will whizz through the stages and have no problem as the time increases. Others may become quite worried and need increases to be in very small increments. Keep watching your puppy's body language to know which type they are and when they're ready to move to the next step.

Step 6 – Adding Distance

This final step is about your distance to the crate. So far, you've been right next to it; now you need to move away so that your puppy can learn to be calm in their crate even when you're not there.

1. Give your puppy the crate cue and close the gate.

2. Now take one step away, step back, and give your pup a treat through the bars.

3. Now take two steps away and again immediately step back and reward.

4. Repeat, adding one step at a time, until you can reach ten steps away.

5. At the ten-step point, change the treat for a longer-lasting chew or treat-filled toy.

6. Over several training sessions, slowly increase your distance from the crate until you can leave the room and finally leave the home.

Reminders for Successful Crate Training

1. The Crate is a Great Place to Be

All the work you're putting in is to help your puppy learn to love their crate. That means that it should never be used as a punishment. Everyone who has owned a puppy will know that there will be times when your patience is really stretched. Ask the pup to go in their crate and provide them with a long-lasting chew. This gives them the chance to calm down and you the opportunity to relax.

2. Don't Use the Crate Excessively

Crates are not suitable for puppies to stay in all day. The Humane Society of the United States[20] suggests that pups under six months of age shouldn't stay in a crate for more than three or four hours at a time. A dog needs human interaction and exercise, so being crated all day and night is going to lead to depression and anxiety problems. Alternatives to this may include a change of schedule, hiring a pet sitter, or using a day care facility.

---

20 https://www.humanesociety.org/resources/crate-training-101

Is Punishment an Effective Way of Changing a Dog's Behavior?

Although positive, reward-based dog training techniques have become much more popular, there still seems to be a tendency to use physical force to stop a dog's unwanted behavior.

Using punishment seems to have grown from assuming that when our dogs misbehave, their aggression is all about dominance. This leads to theories that dog owners need to establish themselves as the "alpha" or "pack leader." Sadly, these ideas persist even though we know that earlier research into the behavior of wolves on which the "pack" theory is based, is probably wrong!

The School of Veterinary Medicine at the University of Pennsylvania wanted to understand what the impact of using punishment was when training dogs. What they found was that it actually increased the dog's aggressive responses. The more aggressive the human was, the more aggressively the dog responded. 43% of dogs who were hit or kicked responded aggressively, while 3% showed an increase in aggression when a corrective sound such as "uh-uh!" was used.

Even 3% is worrying, especially when we know that we can get great results in training while making the process fun for our dogs and without needing to use punishment.

3. **Make Sure Your Pup Has Exercised Before Going into Their Crate**

Your pup is much more likely to settle in their crate if they've had the chance to get rid of some energy first. This also provides them with the opportunity to go to the toilet.

4. **Take Off Your Pup's Collar Before They Go into Their Crate**

Collars are a real choke hazard in a crate where they can get caught, especially when you're not around to free them.

Why Train Your Puppy?

Life with a trained dog is so much more enjoyable. Your dog can be off-leash and enjoy walks where they can run and sniff to their heart's content. You have the peace of mind that when you call them, they'll come running back to you. It means that your dog can patiently wait while you chat with a friend, and it means that you can tell your dog to leave something, and they will.

A trained dog gets much more freedom than an untrained dog. It does take work, and it takes commitment to train regularly. However, the payback comes over the ten plus years of your dog's life. Training a puppy is much easier than training an older dog who has learned bad habits. While a puppy isn't a completely blank slate, you can control much of how they experience life.

We should be realistic in our training. No dog is ever going to be 100% responsive to our requests. Heck, we humans are rarely able to achieve that kind of reliability at work, in sport, or in activities we enjoy. So, it would be unrealistic to expect our dogs to achieve it day in and day out.

Your puppy will also have days where the training just doesn't seem to go as well as it did in the previous session. Maybe they're teething and their gums hurt, or it might be that they're tired from yesterday's activities. Either way, it's not worth damaging the relationship that you've started to develop. Try again tomorrow, and if you're still not getting the results you were expecting, then have a look at our troubleshooting guide at the end of this chapter.

There are several different ways to train the basic control behaviors such as sit and down commands. This chapter is, first of all, going to look at the range of techniques that can be used along with their pros and cons. Then you'll find the guides on how to train the individual behaviors.

Learning theory applies to our puppy and us in much the same way. The promise of a reward motivates us to work harder, whether that's for a bonus at work or the promise of a ticket to a football game. With that in mind, you'll notice that all of the methods are based on what's called positive reinforcement. Victoria Stilwell[21] explains this as your dog learning that "good things happen to him when he does the things you like." The positive refers to adding something to the situation such as food or toys, and the reinforcement means that you want to increase the likelihood of the behavior happening again.

No one wants to use physical force when training their dog, and the great news is that it's just not necessary to get results!

---

21 https://positively.com/dog-training/positive-training/positive-reinforcement/

Reinforcements

Reinforcers are the things that our puppy loves and wants more of. They are the things which tell your pup, "Great job!"

A piece of their dry kibble may work as reinforcement to begin with, but they are likely to get bored with it pretty quickly. A piece of ham or cheese, though, is a whole different situation! And these treats should be tiny; you just want to give enough for your pup to have a taste and want more. You could use a toy, but when you're first training a behavior, you really want to get in several quick repetitions. This helps your puppy to make the connection between offering the behavior and getting the reinforcement. If you're using food, you can probably get three sits completed in ten seconds. If you're using a toy, by the time you give the toy, have a game and then get the toy back again, it's going to take much longer.

If you're thinking, "but I don't want to carry around food or a toy forever," don't worry. The aim is that as your pup develops their knowledge of the behavior, you'll be reducing the use of treats. Instead, we'll be using more verbal "good dogs" along with smiles and strokes. These are also reinforcers, but usually they're not quite as powerful as food and toys for first learning a behavior. There's no better way of speeding up a recall than to offer a tasty treat every now and then!

If you need some inspiration for what you could use as a reinforcer, here's a great list of over 130 ideas![22]

Training for Life

There are two different things to consider here: Firstly, what's important to you, and secondly how training fits into your everyday life.

Every owner has slightly different requirements in terms of what behaviors are important for their puppy to know. If might be that you like to take your pup out with you, so their ability to settle quietly while you chat with friends or have a drink in a café may be a priority. It may be that you love long walks in the hills, so you're aiming for your dog to have a great recall so that they can join you off-leash.

> Ever wondered why Poodles have that weird pom-pom trim?
> Well, the Poodle was originally a hunting dog, and while they were very effective on land, they struggled in the water because of their very dense and curly coat. So, the hunters shaved the Poodle's hindquarters to give them greater flexibility in the water. Then to keep their hip and ankle joints warm, they left them covered in hair. The Poodle's front half was left covered with hair to keep the vital organs warm while they swam in cold water.

---

[22] https://susangarrettdogagility.com/2018/10/reward-list-of-reinforcers/

Then there's thinking about how training fits into everyday life. It can be tough to find time to train when life is already full. That's why you can try to plan training into your routine throughout the day. Asking your pup to lay down while you prepare their breakfast is a great opportunity to build duration to the down behavior in the very distracting environment of their food being prepared. You could also ask your pup to sit when you open the door to the yard. Again, this is an exciting situation in which your pup is learning the self-control needed to offer the sit position, when what they really want to do is to get outside to play. Both of these examples lead to reinforcement for your pup – firstly, getting their breakfast for the down position, and then access to the yard for sitting calmly. When this happens every time they get fed or go outside, your puppy will quickly learn the routine and will soon be throwing themselves into the down position and waiting patiently in a "sit" by the door.

Consistency

When you're consistent, life is so much easier for your pup. Don't forget that your pup is learning all the time, even if you don't think you're training. Every interaction that you have with your puppy provides them with more information on what's required and what the consequences are.

This also applies when you're using cues with your dog. Do you sometimes ask your pup to sit and then they get distracted by something else? Now "sit" doesn't always mean sit. Are there times when you call your puppy even when they are deeply distracted by something, and they don't recall? Now your pup learns to come on the fourth or fifth time you ask them.

Being consistent while setting your pup up for success will result in a keen and eager puppy who loves training and learning new behaviors.

Criteria

Criteria are the steps in your plan of action[23]; they are what you need your puppy to do to get the reinforcement. Before a training session starts, think about what you want to achieve and how it will look. An example of a criterion might be, "my puppy will sit in a "stay" for five seconds."

In each training session, you'll also need to consider whether to increase the criteria to move the behavior closer towards your end goal. A good way of doing this is using the push, stick, or drop method[24].

---

23 https://www.training-your-dog-and-you.com/Criteria.html

24 https://yaletowndogtraining.com/2017/03/07/push-drop-stick-rules-way-make-training-efficient/

How Training Methods Affect the Bond Between You and Your Dog

The world of dog training seems to be divided into two camps: those who use punishment for a dog's failure to respond correctly and those who rely entirely upon rewarding successful behaviors. A team of researchers from the University of Porto considered if the use of punishment when training dogs may affect their emotional attachment to their owners.

They recruited 34 dogs from six different dog training school — three committed to reward-based training, and three which used various types of force or punishments.

To measure the attachment between the dog and its owner, this team used what's called the Strange Situation Test. This measures whether the dog sees the owner as being a "safe haven" after being left alone or with someone that they don't know. Dogs who are securely bonded with their owners are much more willing to explore the room and play with toys scattered around the floor.

The researchers found that dogs trained with reward-based methods played more in the presence of the owner as compared to the stranger, and they greeted and followed the owner more than the stranger. They believed that all those positive interactions that reward-based trainers have with their dogs established the stronger bond; the dog enjoyed being with them. Meanwhile, the dogs trained with punishment had learned that their owners are not necessarily good to be around and may instead be the source of negative feelings.

- Push – If your puppy is successful 4 or 5 times out of 5 then move on to the next stage.

- Stick – If your puppy is successful 3 times out of 5 then repeat that stage.

- Drop – If your puppy is successful 2 or fewer time out of 5 then drop down to an easier stage.

Thinking About Cues

Cues are how your pup knows which behavior you want. So, a cue might be the word "sit," or it could be a whistle for when you want your dog to come back. It could even be a visual cue, so lowering your flat hand towards the floor might mean that you want your puppy to go into a "down." If you're undecided as to whether to go for a verbal, spoken, or visual cue, researchers have identified that dogs are more likely to follow body language cues than spoken ones[25].

This is another area where consistency is essential. If your recall is sometimes cued by saying "here" and other times "come," your puppy will eventually learn both words mean the same thing. However, it will be so much easier for them if there is just one word to learn.

---

[25] https://www.psychologytoday.com/gb/blog/canine-corner/201606/are-voice-commands-or-hand-signals-more-effective-dogs

You will also want to make sure that your cues are all quite different from each other. That means if you use "sit down" to ask for a sit and "lay down" for your puppy to lay flat on the floor then, that could be confusing. "Sit" and "down" would be much clearer.

Once you've decided what the cues will be, make sure that all the family knows what each one is.

Generalizing a Behavior –
Any Time, Any Place, Anywhere!

Puppies are not generally very good at generalizing a behavior when they first learn something new. That means that the context in which they learned it becomes entangled with the behavior. So, a "down" learned in the kitchen, means "down" is offered in the kitchen. A "down" in the living room is something different altogether!

Now the good news is that our dogs get better at generalizing the more training they do. In the early stages of puppy training, you may find that you'll need to take a few steps back in the process when you move to another room or take your training outside.

So, this means that you need to train in lots of different situations so that your youngster understands that the cue means exactly the same no matter where you are. Dog trainer Emily Larlham[26] makes a great point about generalizing, and that's to generalize behaviors to the level you need. There is no need to train a 10-minute "sit-stay" in a busy park if you're never going to need that behavior. Think of what's important to you and your lifestyle.

---

[26] https://dogmantics.com/generalizing/

Techniques

Lure and Reward

This is one of the most common ways of training and is often considered to be one of the quickest and easiest techniques[27]. It involves using something that your puppy really wants, such as a tasty treat, to "lure" them into the behavior you want.

Advantages of Lure and Reward

☺ A quick way of getting a behavior.

☺ An easy technique to understand.

☺ Doesn't require high-level training skills.

---

[27] https://www.dogstardaily.com/training/lure-reward-training

Disadvantages of Lure and Reward

☹ The puppy may just be following the food and not learning.

☹ Without the food, the behavior might not be offered, so that means it needs to be faded out during the training process.

Clicker Training

You may have heard about clicker training, and it may have been discussed as a new training technique, but it's actually been around since the 1940s! Although it didn't become popular in the dog work until the 1990s, the clicker had been used to train all kinds of animals in a huge range of situations, including training pigeons to guide Pelican missiles during World War II[28].

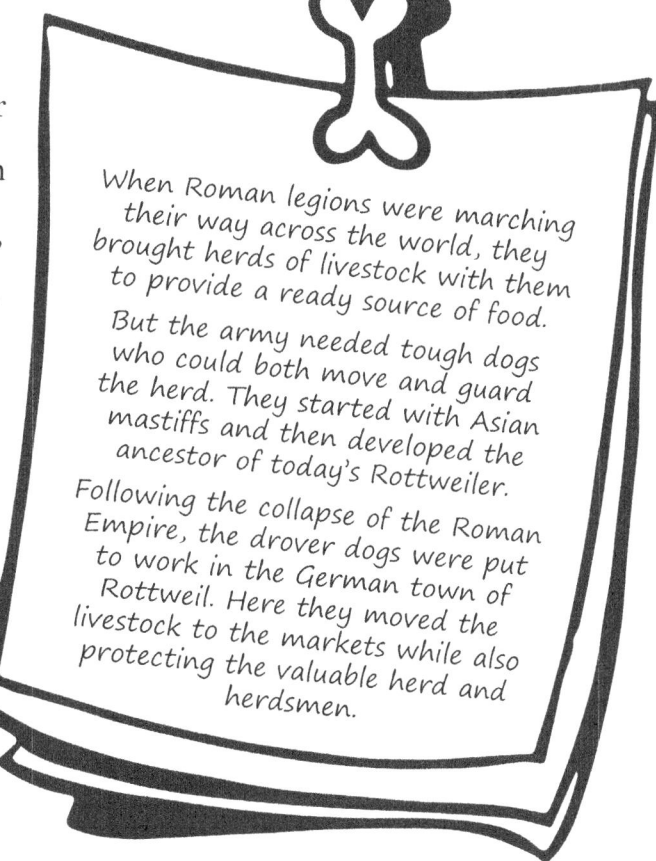

When Roman legions were marching their way across the world, they brought herds of livestock with them to provide a ready source of food.

But the army needed tough dogs who could both move and guard the herd. They started with Asian mastiffs and then developed the ancestor of today's Rottweiler.

Following the collapse of the Roman Empire, the drover dogs were put to work in the German town of Rottweil. Here they moved the livestock to the markets while also protecting the valuable herd and herdsmen.

---

28   https://drsophiayin.com/blog/entry/the-best-animal-trainers-in-history-interview-with-bob-and-marian-bailey/

The clicker is a small plastic mechanical device that costs just a couple of dollars. It makes a short, distinct "click" sound when the button is pressed and that "click" tells your puppy that what they're doing at that exact moment, is the right behavior. The sound also signals to them that reinforcement, usually a treat or a toy, is on its way.

With this technique, the click is a promise which is never broken: "I click, you get rewarded." Now you may be thinking, why not just tell the dog that they were right?

Well, first off, a click can be much more powerful than a spoken word because the only time they hear it is to tell them that "you were right and here comes something good." Whereas your pup hears your voice all day long, when you're speaking on your phone, to your children, even when watching the tv and all those times, your pup learns to ignore your voice.

The click is also very quick and short in sound. That makes it so much easier for you to mark the exact behavior you want. With your voice, by the time you've finished saying "good boy," your pup may no longer be sitting.

Advantages of Clicker Training

☺ A precise way of communicating with your puppy

☺ Provides a consistent message to your pup: click = that was right = treat

Disadvantages of Clicker Training

☹ Requires precise timing to mark the correct behavior

☹ Needs some coordination to manage the clicker and the treats

Target Training

This technique involves teaching your puppy to touch a body part to a specific object. That could be their nose, paw, or even their chin. Training your pet to touch a target is not only a fun game to play, but it's also easy to teach. As an added bonus, it's also a perfect way to teach the behaviors needed for vet checks and grooming.

Most people start by teaching their dog how to target with their nose towards a target stick. This can then be used to guide the puppy into position. If you have a small dog, targeting can also be an excellent way of avoiding being bent over double, which is what would happen if you tried to lure them!

Targeting is introduced by first of all letting your dog investigate the target with their nose. When they make contact, take a piece of food from your pocket and reward. It doesn't take many repetitions before your pup is pushing their nose to the target as quickly as they can!

Can Dogs Recognize Emotions Just by Looking at Our Faces?

When you look over to someone, you can probably get a pretty good idea of how they're feeling based on their facial expression. But what about dogs? Can they do the same?

The Messerli Research Institute at the University of Veterinary Medicine in Vienna has been looking into whether this might be the case. Eleven dogs were trained to recognize the difference between a happy face or an angry one by being shown either the upper or the lower half of a person's face. Then it was decided whether the dog would be rewarded for indicating whenever they saw a happy or angry face shown on the computer display. All the dog had to do was to touch the screen with their noses and when they were correct, they were given a food reward.

To make sure the dogs hadn't just learned which face resulted in a food reward, the dogs were shown either the other half of the face used in the training stage or the images of people's faces they hadn't seen before. The researchers found that the dogs could still tell the difference between the happy and angry expressions.

The study demonstrated that dogs could distinguish between angry and happy expressions in humans, even in people they had never met before.

One extra, important fact identified from the research was that the dogs were much slower to learn that an angry face could mean a reward during the training stage of the study. This seemed to show that the dogs already knew that it's best to stay away from people when they look angry. So, asking the dogs to approach and touch the angry face to get a reward initially caused confusion. So, that means you should definitely avoid training your dog if you're not feeling in a good mood!

Now, this may sound very similar to lure and reward, but it has a key advantage. Remember the treat that came from your pocket? That meant that there were no visible treats which can be distracting for dogs who are food lovers. For these guys, being able to see the food means that they struggle to learn because they're just thinking "Food! Follow the food!"

Introducing this method can be combined with the clicker to mark the exact moment your pup's nose makes contact. As with any training technique, problems can happen when we don't think things through in advance. Dog trainer Eileen Fletcher[29] talks about how she "messed up" her dog's target training so that you can avoid falling into the same traps.

Advantages of Target Training

☺ Because the food is hidden right from the start, you don't need to fade it in the way you have to with lure and reward.

☺ A great way of teaching all kinds of behaviors and tricks including "go to your bed" and weaving between your legs.

---

[29] https://eileenanddogs.com/blog/2013/08/30/hand-target/

Disadvantages of Target Training

☹ Coordination needed to manage the target stick, retrieving the treat from your pocket and potentially a clicker as well.

☹ Need to fade out the target so that your pup can still perform the behavior when it's not there.

Training the Behaviors

"Sit"

This is such a useful behavior to have and one which, for many dogs, becomes what's called a default behavior. The default behavior is usually one of the first ones you taught your pup, and so has had heaps of reinforcement. This means that if they're not sure what's needed, they will sit, which is no bad thing!

A sit command is an excellent option to prevent behaviors you don't want, such as jumping up at the counter when you're preparing their food. It also means that they can meet people politely, with all paws on the floor. The "sit" also avoids crazy excited behavior when you're trying to clip on their leash to go for a walk.

Teaching a "Sit" with Lure and Reward

1. Hold a tasty treat between finger and thumb.

2. With your puppy standing, show them the treat and move it just above their nose.

3. Keeping the treat close to their nose, move it back over their body.

4. As your pup lifts their head back to follow the treat, their bottom goes down and into a "sit."

5. Reward with the treat.

6. Repeat five times.

7. Once you're pretty sure that your pup will go into the "sit" when you lure them, say your cue word, such as "sit," as their bottom hits the floor.

8. Repeat five times.

Fading out the lure

1. Now use exactly the same hand movement but with no treat between your fingers.

2. As soon as your pup sits, grab a treat from your pocket, and reward.

3. Repeat five times, with every "sit" being rewarded with a treat from your pocket.

Fading out the hand movement

1. Repeat five more times, but each time make the hand movement a little smaller.

2. Finally, without any hand movement, just use your cue word to ask for the sit behavior and then reward.

Tip – If your pup jumps up, the treat is too high, move it back to just above their nose.

Teaching a "Sit" with Clicker Training

1. With a treat in your hand, sit on the floor with your pup.

2. The moment they sit, click, and then reward.

3. Throw a treat across the floor for your pup to chase and get them out of the "sit."

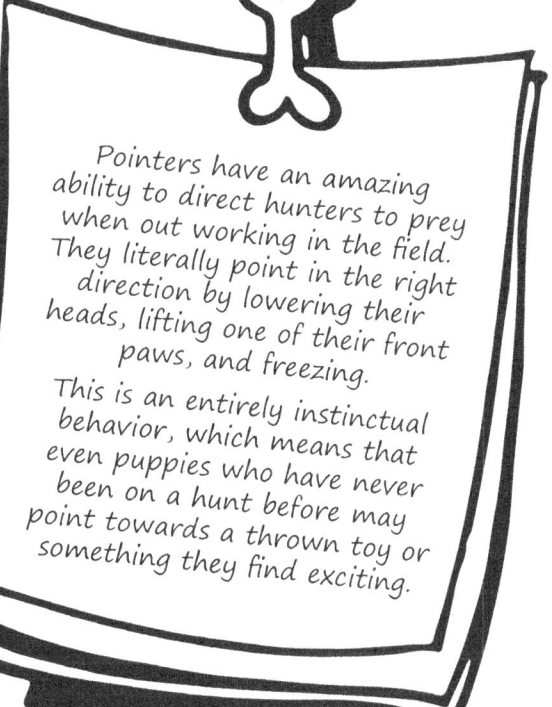

Pointers have an amazing ability to direct hunters to prey when out working in the field. They literally point in the right direction by lowering their heads, lifting one of their front paws, and freezing.

This is an entirely instinctual behavior, which means that even puppies who have never been on a hunt before may point towards a thrown toy or something they find exciting.

4. Wait for them to sit again, click, then reward.

5. Repeat five times.

6. If your puppy is quickly sitting again and waiting for their treat, say your cue word, and when your pup sits, click and then reward.

7. Repeat five times.

8. Say your cue word and then provide your pup with the treat.

Teaching a "Sit" with Target Training

To use this technique, you need to have already provided lots of rewards for your puppy investigating and then touching the end of the target stick with their nose.

1. With your puppy standing, move the target stick towards their nose and let them offer their touch.

2. Keeping the target stick close to their nose, slowly move it back over their body.

3. As your pup lifts their head back to follow the target, their bottom goes down and into a "sit."

4. Reward with a treat.

5. Repeat five times.

6. Once you're pretty sure that your pup will go into the sit, say your cue word, such as "sit," as you present the target stick.

7. Repeat five times.

Fading out the target stick

1. Repeat five more times, but each time increase the distance between your pup's nose and the target stick.

2. Without any use of the target stick, use your cue word to ask for the sit behavior.

"Down"

Down command is a great option for when you need your pup to be a little more settled and chilled out. Now, it can sometimes be more challenging to teach a small breed puppy to lie down, but we've included some extra ideas, just for you, at the end of this section.

Would Your Dog Try to Rescue You?

Have you ever wondered if your dog would respond like Lassie? If you were trapped in a box and crying for help, would your dog try to set you free?

That's precisely what researchers from Arizona State University tried to find out! They assessed 60 pet dogs to see if they would rescue their owners who had been confined to a large box with a lightweight door that the dogs could move aside. Meanwhile, the owners were asked to pretend that they were distressed by calling out "help" and "help me" but were told not to use the dog's name as the researchers didn't want the dog to act out of obedience.

They found that around one-third of the dogs rescued their owners. When they replaced the owners with the dogs seeing food being placed in the box, only 19 dogs opened the door to get to the tasty treats. So that means that more dogs rescued their owners than retrieved food!

Finally, the researchers checked to see what happened when the owner sat inside the box and calmly read aloud from a magazine. Then, only 16 out of 60 dogs opened the box.

So, it does seem that when our dogs think we're distressed, they can have their very own "Lassie moment"!

Teaching a "Down" with Lure and Reward – Technique 1

1. Hold a tasty treat held between finger and thumb.

2. With your puppy sitting, show them the treat and hold it at the end of their nose.

3. Keeping the treat close to their nose, move it down to the floor, to just behind their paws.

4. As your pup lowers their head, hold the treat in a fist on the floor.

5. Once they have gone all the way down, you can reward with the treat.

6. Repeat five times.

7. Once you're pretty sure that your pup will go into the "down" when you lure them, say your cue word, such as "down," as they get into position.

8. Repeat five times.

Fading out the lure

1. Now use exactly the same hand movement but with no treat between your fingers.

2. As soon as your pup goes into the "down", grab a treat from your pocket and reward.

3. Repeat five times, with every "down" being rewarded with a treat from your pocket.

Fading out the hand movement

1. Repeat five more times, but each time make the hand movement a little smaller.

2. Finally, without any hand movement, just use your cue word to ask for the down behavior and then reward.

Teaching a "Down" with Lure and Reward – Technique 2

1. With a treat in your hand, sit on the floor with your pup.

2. Now keep the treat in a closed fist and place it on the floor.

3. As your puppy investigates, wait for them to go into the "down".

4. The moment they go into the "down," reward.

5. Repeat five times.

6. Once you're pretty sure that your pup will go into the "down" when you lure them, say your cue word, such as "down," as they get into position.

7. Repeat five times.

Then, repeat the fading out of the lure and the hand movement the same as for the first technique.

Teaching a "Down" with Clicker Training

This way of teaching the down command is exactly the same way as technique 2, but you'll be clicking the moment your pup goes into the down position.

Teaching a "Down" with Target Training

To use this technique, you need to have already provided lots of rewards for your puppy investigating and then touching the end of the target stick with their nose.

1. With your puppy standing, move the target stick towards their nose and let them offer their touch.

2. Keeping the target stick close to their nose, slowly move it down to the floor and just behind their paws.

3. As your pup drops their head to follow the target, their body goes into a "down."

4. Reward with the treat.

5. Repeat five times.

6. Once you're pretty sure that your pup will go into the "down," say your cue word, such as "down," as they lay flat on the floor.

7. Repeat five times.

Fading out the target stick

1. Repeat five more times, but each time increase the distance between your pup's nose and the target stick.

2. Without any use of the target stick, use your cue word to ask for the down behavior.

Tips for Teaching a "Down" to a Small Dog

Training small dogs to go down can be tricky. This might be because they are already so low to the ground that the lure doesn't go far from their nose down to the ground. That then makes it difficult for them to understand what it is that you want.

One method which is often very successful is:

1. Sit on the floor and have one leg stretched out in front.

2. Then, bend your knee to create an upside-down "V" shape.

3. With a tasty treat, lure your puppy under your knee, which should be a little lower than the height of your pups back.

4. As they crouch to go under, reward any behavior which requires your pup to get lower to the floor.

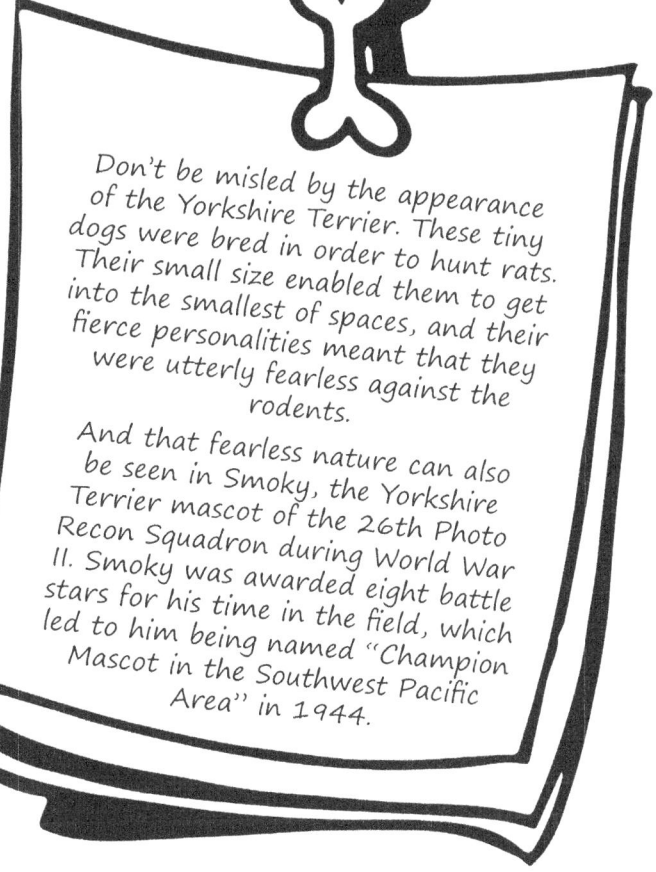

Don't be misled by the appearance of the Yorkshire Terrier. These tiny dogs were bred in order to hunt rats. Their small size enabled them to get into the smallest of spaces, and their fierce personalities meant that they were utterly fearless against the rodents.

And that fearless nature can also be seen in Smoky, the Yorkshire Terrier mascot of the 26th Photo Recon Squadron during World War II. Smoky was awarded eight battle stars for his time in the field, which led to him being named "Champion Mascot in the Southwest Pacific Area" in 1944.

5. Slowly lower your knee height before each repetition and until your pup needs to go flat down to get the treat.

Recall

This is the behavior that will change your dog's life forever. When a dog has a great recall, they have a freedom that's just not possible for a leashed dog. Now they can play with other dogs, sniff and explore and you don't need to worry about whether they will come back. Behaviorist and trainer Kathy Sdao[30] describes having a reliable recall as having "the ability to saves dogs' lives and owners' sanity!"

A recall is a behavior that is in training throughout your dog's life. The environment, when out on a walk, changes all the time, and that can create some real challenges in their ability to listen and recall. Don't be stingy with your reinforcement; to keep that recall sharp and quickly responded to, reward each time your pup comes to you when asked. Sometimes it might be a fuss and lots of praise, other times it might be a really good treat such as cooked chicken. Your pup has left something which was probably really interesting to come to you when asked – that needs rewarding!

Once you've selected a technique and followed the steps, you can then begin to extend the distance between you and your pup. At the end of this section, you'll also

---

30 http://www.kathysdao.com/articles/the-first-steps-to-reliable-recall/

find the recall game to help strengthen the behavior and involve family and friends in training.

Teaching a Recall with Lure and Reward

1. Show your pup that you have a treat in your hand.

2. Keeping the treat at your pup's nose height, take a few steps backward.

3. As your pups comes towards you, offer the treat.

4. Repeat five times.

5. Once you're pretty sure that your pup will follow the treat as you step backward, say your cue word, such as "come," as they step towards you.

6. Repeat five times.

Fading out the lure

1. Now use exactly the same hand movement but with no treat between your fingers.

2. As soon as your pup comes in close, grab a treat from your pocket and reward.

3. Repeat five times, with every recall being rewarded with a treat from your pocket.

Fading out the hand movement

1. Repeat five more times, but rather than the treat being close to your pup's nose, bring it in a little closer to you.

2. Gradually bring your hand in closer and closer with each repetition.

3. Finally, without any hand movement, just use your cue word to ask for the recall as you step backward and then reward.

Teaching a Recall with Clicker Training

1. With your pup close by, take a few steps backward.

2. As soon as your pup comes towards you, click and then treat.

> Did you know that the Labrador is the most popular breed in America? And that they've been in the top 10 rankings since the 1970s?
>
> But that's no surprise when you consider their amazing adaptability. From guide dog for the blind to detection dog for explosives and drugs, the Labrador can truly turn their paw to whatever job we ask them to complete.
>
> That Labrador popularity isn't restricted to the United States either. They are also the most popular breed in the UK, and they feature in the top 10 in many other countries, including Australia, Italy, and Canada.

3. Repeat five times.

4. Once you're pretty sure that your pup will follow the treat as you step backward, say your cue word, such as "come," as they step towards you.

5. Repeat five times.

Training a Recall with Target Training

So far, you've been using a target stick for your dog to touch their nose towards. For the recall, you might find it useful to teach a hand touch instead. This means that if you're out and about, you can practice the recall without needing the target stick; an arm stretched out can be a really effective visual cue for your puppy to run towards.

A hand touch is taught in exactly the same way as you introduced the target stick:

1. Hold out your hand, and as your puppy investigates it with their nose, praise and reward.

2. Repeat five times or until it becomes clear that your pup understands a nose touch = food.

3. Swap hands, so if using your left, now swap to your right hand and repeat five times.

4. Now change the height of your hand, down low to the ground, and high enough that your pup needs to reach up to get their touch in.

5. Repeat several times.

Now you're ready to use the hand touch in recall training:

1. Ask your puppy to touch your outstretched hand with their nose.

2. Take a step back and ask for a nose touch.

3. As your puppy steps forward and touches, praise and reward.

4. Repeat five times.

5. Once you're pretty sure that your pup will follow you and nose touch your hand, you can add the cue word, such as "come," as they move towards you.

6. Repeat five times.

There is no need to fade out the hand touch for the recall, as it can continue to be your cue for your puppy to come back to you.

Puppy Recall Game

This is an excellent game for the family to play and one which we've found children love being involved in. Don't forget in all the fun that you should still be aiming for your pup to be as successful as possible. So, if the game does become too exciting, you may need to make it easier for them to go to the right person.

Level 1 – two people needed

1. The two people who are playing need to stand around 20 feet away from each other and have a supply of tasty treats.

2. Each person takes it in turn to call the pup and reward them for coming.

3. If the puppy gets stuck with one person, the second person should run up to them, show the pup the treat, and run back to their position.

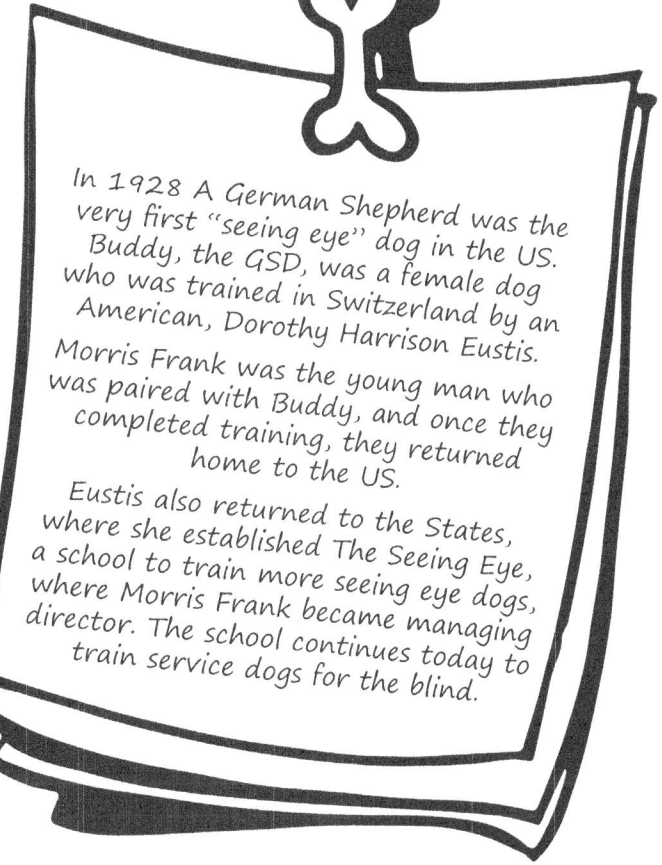

In 1928 A German Shepherd was the very first "seeing eye" dog in the US. Buddy, the GSD, was a female dog who was trained in Switzerland by an American, Dorothy Harrison Eustis. Morris Frank was the young man who was paired with Buddy, and once they completed training, they returned home to the US.

Eustis also returned to the States, where she established The Seeing Eye, a school to train more seeing eye dogs, where Morris Frank became managing director. The school continues today to train service dogs for the blind.

4. Practice 10 times with your puppy going back and forth.

Level 2 - three people needed

1. Have the three people in a triangle shape about 20 ft from each other and with a supply of tasty treats.

2. Each person takes it in turn to call the puppy as they move clockwise around the triangle.

3. Now go counterclockwise around the triangle.

4. Now go out of order to make sure your puppy is listening and not making educated guesses! So that might be:

    a. Person 1 - Person 2

    b. Person 2 - Person 1

    c. Person 1 - Person 3

    d. Person 3 - Person 1

    e. Person 1 - Person 2

"Stay"

Before we begin to start working on the "stay," let's first talk about the difference between a "stay" and a "settle." A "stay" is a more formal behavior. It means don't move, stay in position until I give the release word for you to move or ask you to do something else. The "settle" means I need you to chill out and relax. It's okay if you get up and turn around to get more comfortable as long as you stay in roughly the same space.

Coming back to the release word for a moment. This is a cue that tells your pup that the stay behavior has now finished, and they can get up and move. It could be something like "finish" or "all done."

There are three elements to training a "stay," which the AKC describes as being duration, distance, and distractions[31].

- Duration relates to how long your puppy can remain in the "stay" without moving.

- Distance is how far away you are from your puppy, while they stay in position.

- Distractions are the things that will pull their attention away from the job at hand and tempt them to break the "stay."

---

[31] https://www.akc.org/expert-advice/training/dog-training-duration-distance-distraction/

Each of the three "Ds" needs to be trained separately so that your puppy develops an excellent understanding of what's required.

Training a "Stay" with Lure and Reward

So, we hit some problems trying to use lure and reward for training a "stay." That's because when you start to add any distance, you won't be able to carry on luring unless you have very long arms!

The other challenge comes from having a very foody dog who will want to follow you because you have great things to eat in your hand. So, for this behavior, we recommend using target training or clicker training.

Golden Retrievers have several entries in the Guinness Book of Records.

Firstly, there is Finley, the Golden Retriever who has claimed the record for holding the most tennis balls in their mouth at the same time. Finley can fit in an incredible six! It seems he likes to retrieve a ball when thrown but isn't so keen to let it go, and that's how he managed to achieve this awesome record!

Then there is Augie, the oldest Golden Retriever in the world! Augie reached an incredible 20 years of age in 2020.

The unofficial record for the most Golden Retrievers all gathered together in one place? Well, that would be 681 at a Golden Retriever event held in California, on October 14, 2018.

Training a "Stay" with Clicker Training

Duration is the first D to work on. Remember to click and reward after every repetition when your puppy is successful and use the push, stick, drop technique to decide when to move to the next step.

1. Stand right in front of your dog, count to two, click and then reward.

2. Repeat, adding one second at a time until you reach ten seconds.

3. Now add two seconds at a time until you reach twenty seconds.

4. Finally, add 5 seconds at a time until you reach 60 seconds.

Now we can work on distance:

1. Standing in front of your dog, take one step backward and immediately come back, click and reward.

2. Repeat three times.

3. Now repeat steps 1 and 2 but add one step each time until you reach ten paces.

Finally, you can work on distractions. When we add in distractions, we need to make the other Ds easier to increase the opportunity for the puppy to be successful. Distractions might include:

- Walking out of the room and back in.

- Walking around your pup.

- Holding a toy and dropping it to the floor.

- Dropping a piece of food on the floor.

- Someone else coming into the room.

Remember not to set your puppy up to fail; you want them to be right so that you can reinforce and make that behavior even stronger. That means you may need to break down some of those distractions to make them easier to begin with.

Training a "Stay" with Target Training

So far, we've used a nose target, but targeting could be the puppy touching any part of their body to an object. For teaching a "stay," we're going to use a mat on the floor which your pup is going to target their "sit" or "down" to. To make things easier for your puppy, avoid using their bed. We want the mat to have one meaning, and that's to stay on it until you hear the release word. The first steps are all about making the mat a very rewarding place to be.

1. Place the mat on the floor, and as your pup comes over to investigate, throw a piece of food onto the mat.

2. As they wander off, again toss a piece of food onto the mat.

3. Repeat several times until your pup is hanging around on the mat waiting for the next treat.

Now, you can check understanding by throwing a treat a few feet away and then waiting to see if your pup runs back to the mat, waiting for the next one. Once you can see that your pup thinks that the mat is the best place ever to hang out, you can work on the three Ds in the same way as for the clicker training method.

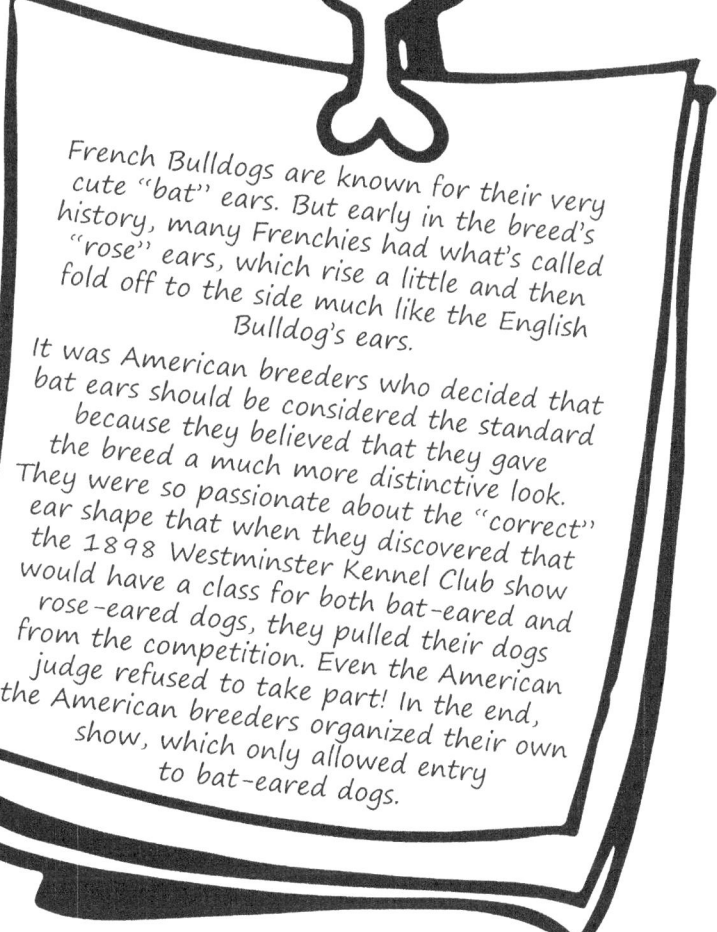

French Bulldogs are known for their very cute "bat" ears. But early in the breed's history, many Frenchies had what's called "rose" ears, which rise a little and then fold off to the side much like the English Bulldog's ears.

It was American breeders who decided that bat ears should be considered the standard because they believed that they gave the breed a much more distinctive look. They were so passionate about the "correct" ear shape that when they discovered that the 1898 Westminster Kennel Club show would have a class for both bat-eared and rose-eared dogs, they pulled their dogs from the competition. Even the American judge refused to take part! In the end, the American breeders organized their own show, which only allowed entry to bat-eared dogs.

"Leave It"

This is such an important cue to have when your puppy steals something they shouldn't, such as your wallet or purse. It can also be used when they go to eat something revolting in the park or, even worse, go towards something which might be poisonous for them to eat or dangerous to be near.

One important consideration for the "leave it" cue is that it's not to punish your puppy. It's simply telling them that they should leave that and get something better over here. The Guide Dog Foundation[32] reminds us that even their well-trained dogs can get distracted because of their active and intrigued minds.

When you get angry, your puppy is less likely to want to come back to you, and in a situation where they might be in danger that's the last thing you want to happen. So, no matter which technique you decide to use, there's no need to say "no" or anything else which tells your pup off for investigating. The purpose of this exercise is for them to learn that the "leave it" cue is an awesome one to hear because it means that they get great stuff to eat.

---

[32] https://www.guidedog.org/PuppyRaising/PuppyRaiserManual/PuppyDevelopment/Teaching_Leave_It_Verbal_Cue.aspx

Training the "Leave It" Using Lure and Reward

For this exercise, you need two types of food. Firstly, something boring, which might be dry popcorn or some stale bread or plain pasta; and then some delicious food, which might be cooked chicken, ham, or cheese. It's also easier to train the "leave it" if you can be down on the floor close to your pup.

Stage 1

1. Place a piece of boring food onto the floor, and cover it with your hand.

2. As your pup comes to investigate, lure them away with the great food in your other hand.

3. Give your puppy the great food when they're an arm's length from the boring food.

4. Uncover the boring food and let them again approach it.

5. Again, lure them away with the great food in your other hand and feed them at arm's length.

6. This time as your pup comes to investigate, use your "leave it" cue, which could be "leave it" or "off."

7. Again, lure them away with the great food in your other hand and feed them at arm's length.

You're ready for the next stage when your puppy looks for the good food when you give your "leave it" cue.

Stage 2

Now we move on to the generalization stage, so that means moving from the boring food to other objects. For this level, select household items you don't want your puppy to have. Remember you need to be able to hold them in your fist or cover them with a box to make sure your pup can't get them while they are still learning what "leave it" means, you don't want a tug-of-war situation!

Now you can follow the same steps from stage 1 to help your puppy understand that the "leave it" cue applies to all kinds of different situations.

> Ever wondered why the Bulldog has all those wrinkles? Well, first off back in their days of bull-baiting, there was the risk that the blood that flew around would get into the dog's eyes and prevent them from fighting at their best. With the wrinkles in place, the blood was blocked from getting into the dog's eyes.
>
> The wrinkles also provided the Bulldog with some protection against other dogs. That's because if they were attacked, the loose folds of their skin helped to prevent the Bulldog from receiving a serious injury.

Training the "Leave It" Using Clicker Training

1. Hold the boring food in your closed fist and then let your puppy investigate it.

2. The moment their nose comes away from your fist, click and then reward with the good food.

3. Repeat until your pup decides that it's more rewarding to come away from the boring food.

4. Now, open your fist, and the moment your pup steps forward, close it again.

5. The moment their nose comes away from your fist, click, and then reward.

6. Repeat until you can open your hand right up, and your pup waits for the good food to appear.

7. Once you are sure that your pup will not approach the boring food, you can add in your "leave it" cue.

Remember, no telling the puppy "no." Instead, let them work out what causes the great food to appear; then, you have a behavior that will be performed with speed and enthusiasm.

Training the "Leave It" Using Target Training

You could ask your dog to touch your hand instead of investigating the item you don't want them to have. However, that's probably not going to be the most reliable way of encouraging a puppy away from something that they perceive as being really good. So, for this one, lure and reward or clicker training are your best options.

Trouble Shooting

When training isn't going as planned, our troubleshooting guide will soon get you back on track.

😕 Increasing the Difficulty Too Quickly

Training a puppy is like building a house: you need to have solid foundations to build upon. When we make the behavior too difficult too quickly, then we don't have that foundation in place. So, this might happen if we are teaching the pup a "stay." Perhaps they were successful at staying for five seconds, and then we leaped to 10 seconds. After eight seconds, our puppy gets up and moves around. This just tells us that right now, our pup can only safely stay for seven seconds. For the next few repetitions, we'll just ask for seven seconds and then build up one second at a time to 10.

😕 The Environment Changed

Remember that pups aren't great at generalizing their behavior. Back up a few steps in the training process when you move your training somewhere new. They will soon have the "aha" moment of understanding that this is just the same as before, and they'll be quickly offering you the right behavior.

😐 Too Distracting

Puppies are a little like small children in that they can become distracted very, very quickly. Did someone walk into the room? A loud noise on the television? A leaf blowing in the wind? All enough for their attention to be drawn away from the task at hand. You can make it easier for your pup to learn by training in a very non-distracting environment to begin with and then moving well-known behaviors to more challenging situations.

This is a breed that probably shouldn't be on your shortlist if you live in an apartment. That's because they are well known for being one of the most vocal breeds!

Now, there is a reason for this, and that's because when they are hunting, they will begin to "bay" to let their human companions know they are on the trail of the fox.

However, the Beagle doesn't only bay, they also bark and howl. But then they are simply true to their name, and that's because "Beagle" is believed to come from the French term "bee gueule," which means wide throat or loud mouth.

😐 Puppy's Not Interested in Training

We all have days where we feel a little less motivated than others, and there's no reason to suspect that it's any different for our pups. This might be because they are tired from a poor night's sleep, perhaps they feel a little under the weather, or maybe yesterday was really busy or stressful, and they've still not completely recovered. However, if this carries on for more than a few days, we need to work out what's going on.

Here's our checklist to work through:

- 🦴 Consider the quality of the reinforcer. Are you using something a bit boring like kibble? Try something more interesting such as cheese or cooked meats instead.

- 🦴 Have you had a training session where your pup got more things wrong than they did right? That's not going to be very rewarding or much fun. Keep things easy for a couple of sessions, focus on lots of reinforcement and bringing the fun back to training.

- 🦴 Are you feeling tired or stressed or unwell? When we're not feeling ourselves, it's tough to be upbeat with our pups. Give yourself a break for a few days and focus on games and bonding time on the sofa instead.

Training Your Puppy to Walk on a Loose Leash

One of the real joys of having a dog is going for walks together. However, when a dog is pulling on the leash, it just takes all the pleasure out of what should be a relaxing time together. If there is one situation in which it's important not to reward a behavior you don't want, it's loose leash walking. If your puppy discovers that by pulling they can get to go where they want to be quicker than by having a loose leash, it's going to be a battle to then convince them otherwise.

Now, you will have several weeks between when your pup arrives at home with you and when they have finished their vaccinations and can go out for a walk. So, that provides the perfect opportunity to start leash training in the nice quiet environment of your home.

Getting Organized for Training Loose Leash Walking

It is completely possible to train all sizes and ages of dogs to walk on a loose leash without needing to inflict discomfort or pain. E-collars, prong collars, choke chains, all rely on causing pain to convince your puppy to walk with you. And while pain avoidance is a strong motivator, you have to ask yourself if the only reason your puppy is walking with you is to avoid pain, is that really the relationship you imagined having with your dog?

Yes, it will take a little longer to train loose leash walking without using pain; but that investment in time will last your pup's whole life, and you'll have a stronger, more positive relationship because of it.

Many owners now walk their dogs in a harness rather than a collar. Although you might associate a harness with dogs pulling, there's no need for that to be the case. If a puppy is going to pull on a walk, it'll happen whether they're wearing a harness or a collar!

What we do know is that there are far fewer risks to your pup's wellbeing from being walked in a harness rather than a collar. Dr. Peter Dobias DVM[33] has written about

> The name "Poodle" comes from the German word, "pudel," which means "to splash." In Germany, the Poodle is called the Pudelhund.
>
> This is a perfect name for a dog that was used to retrieve waterfowl from the water for the hunters.
>
> Standard Poodles, the largest of the three sizes, are very capable of working in the field. Since the United Kennel Club launched their retriever hunt tests in 1984, several standard poodles have earned the highest titles. The North American Hunting Retriever Association also considers the Poodle a retriever breed, and as such, they are allowed to take part in their retriever field tests.

---

[33] https://peterdobias.com/blogs/blog/11015137-choke-prong-and-shock-collars-can-irreversibly-damage-your-dog

how choke, prong, and shock collars can irreversibly damage your dog, and top trainer Emily Larlham[34] discusses how they can cause pain and suffering.

Alongside the harness, you'll also need a leash. For training loose leash walking in the house, look for one that's cheap and lightweight. In this situation, it's not being used for safety, and it will be easier for your pup to get used to something which isn't too heavy to start with. Once you're ready to move outside the home, then a stronger leash will be needed.

You'll also need lots of small and tasty treats or a favorite toy if your puppy is more motivated by that than food.

Traditionally, dogs have walked on the left-hand side of their owner, and this has come across from the world of gundogs. That's because the hunter would usually carry their gun draped across the crook of their right arm, so it was easier to keep the dog on the left-hand side. However, there is no reason why your puppy can't walk on your right-hand side or indeed learn how to walk on either side! You might also want to consider where your first walks will be and which side will keep your youngster furthest away from traffic.

---

[34] https://dogmantics.com/is-it-harmful-to-attach-a-leash-to-your-dogs-neck-2/

Leash Training

Now, this may sound a little odd, but we're going to start leash training with no leash. Why? Well, the moment we put a leash onto a puppy, there's a pretty good chance that they will run to the end of it and create tension, and that's the last thing we want to happen. So instead, you're going to teach your pup the right position to be in without the leash. This is all about teaching strong foundations, an approach which trainer Nan Arthur[35] says is about being willing to start at step one and progress slowly.

You'll find the section on adding in the leash after the methods for teaching the correct position have been discussed.

As ever, there is more than one way to teach a behavior. All of the techniques we spoke about earlier in the book can be used to teach loose leash walking, so that's lure and reward, clicker training, and targeting. The two methods described below combine some of these techniques to help your puppy understand what's required for this behavior.

Method One – Follow the Food

1. Start in a small area that has no distractions, such as a hallway.

---

[35] https://www.clickertraining.com/loose-leash-walking-part-one

2. If you want your puppy to walk on your left, grab a bowl of food and hold it in your right hand. If walking your pup on the right-hand side, hold the bowl in your left hand. Having the bowl on the opposite side means you still have your pup's interest but it reduces the tendency to jump up.

3. With your puppy off-leash, take a few paces forward.

4. Your pup's interest in the food will encourage them to follow you. If they're not sure, you can tap your leg to encourage them closer or turn your body so that it faces more towards them.

5. Make changes in direction to keep your pup guessing and in the right position.

6. Aim for two or three turns and then reward success with access to the food bowl.

Rottweilers have an undeserved reputation for being fearsome dogs. While they were bred as guard dogs and do retain a guarding instinct, in the right hands, they are a fantastic and trustworthy breed.

In fact, Wynd, a Rottweiler therapy dog, won the Award for Canine Excellence in Therapy in 2015. Wynd was a therapy dog with The Tragedy Assistance Program for Survivors.

Then there is Dieter, another Rottweiler service dog who helps Vietnam veteran, Neil Williams. Neil suffered a spinal injury during the war, and Dieter helps him with all kinds of tasks, including assisting him in getting in and out of his wheelchair.

7. Short sessions are the aim here, so don't put all your pup's food in the bowl in one go. Instead, you could repeat this with four mini-meals before making the 5th one a larger meal to finish up on.

For this method, you'll need to fade out the presence of the bowl, as you don't want your pup to think that they only need to offer a nice heel position when you have a bowl of food in your hand! To do this:

1. Complete one repetition with the bowl in your hand.

2. Once your pup has eaten from the bowl, show them that you have some more food only this time, it's in your hand.

3. Then set off in precisely the same way as you have done before, with your hand in the same position as it would have been when holding the bowl.

4. Repeat over several days.

Now you need to fade out your hand position and the food "lure" so that your pup can still be in the right place without needing to see the food:

1. Complete one repetition with food in your hand as before.

2. Now keep your hand in the same position but this time without any food. Take a few steps, make a turn, and then give your pup a treat taken from your pocket.

3. Repeat several times.

4. Now begin to move your hand from the position it's been in back to your side. This may take several repetitions to complete this stage slowly and so that it doesn't seem like too much of a change to your pup.

5. Finally, you have a pup who walks nicely by your side. Now you can add in your cue word, which might be "heel" or "close."

Method Two – The Reward Zone

This method focusses on teaching your puppy the right place to be, before adding in any movement.

1. Stand close to a wall, so there is just enough space for your puppy to get in-between.

2. With a treat, lure your puppy into position by your side and then reward.

3. Throw another treat across the floor for your pup to chase.

4. As they come back to you, lure them with a treat into position between you and the wall.

5. Repeat five times.

6. Next time, lure pup to the right position but without food in your hand.

7. Repeat five times.

To move to the next stage, your puppy should be coming back into position by your side without needing to be lured.

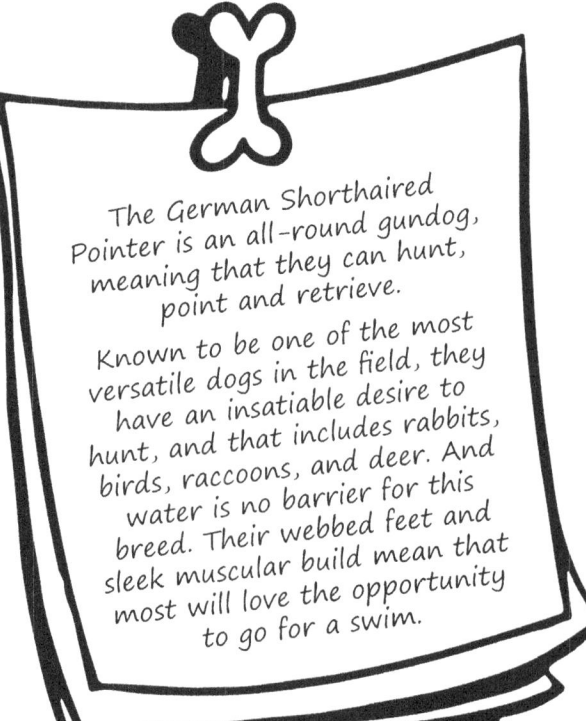

The German Shorthaired Pointer is an all-round gundog, meaning that they can hunt, point and retrieve.
Known to be one of the most versatile dogs in the field, they have an insatiable desire to hunt, and that includes rabbits, birds, raccoons, and deer. And water is no barrier for this breed. Their webbed feet and sleek muscular build mean that most will love the opportunity to go for a swim.

1. With pup in position between you and the wall, take a step forward.

2. Stop and wait for your pup to move forward into the right spot.

3. Reward and repeat five times.

4. Slowly build up to being able to complete five steps, all with your pup in the correct position.

5. Now take a step away from the wall to create a larger gap.

6. Lure pup into position with food if needed and then slowly build up to five paces.

Once your pup can complete five paces away from the wall, they are showing that they understand the best place to be is by your side! Now you need to practice in different rooms, starting off close to the wall and then once more moving further away.

Introducing the Leash

So, your pup is now happily walking by your side through turns and changes of pace and in several different locations. Now is the time to add in the leash.

One of the reasons for not using it earlier was to avoid your puppy flying to the end of it before they understood the position they should be in. Another reason was to prevent the temptation for you to pull against the leash, creating tension. You now know that your pup can walk very nicely by your side and that there is no need to use any pressure for that to happen.

Step One

Clip the leash onto your pup's harness, then tuck the handle end of the leash into your waistband. Why? Well, having it there means that you can't pull on it!

Then go back to an earlier stage in the method you used. This is because the situation has changed, and your pup may be curious about this new "thing." If they attempt to grab the leash in their teeth, you then have treats in your hand, to distract them with instead.

Step Two

Now you can repeat step one, but this time holding the leash in your hand. This is different again for your pup, as they might feel a little tension from time to time. So, take that step back in the process again and keep food in your hand for several repetitions.

Aim for your puppy to be able to:

🦮 Walk nicely on the leash in different locations around the home and yard.

🦮 Stay in a close position when you turn and walk in a new direction.

🦮 Hold position when you adjust your pace from slow to fast and normal.

Ongoing Loose Leash Training

Retain the Element of Surprise!

Every now and then, on each walk, surprise your pup by rewarding them for their loose leash walking. This might be by pulling out a hidden toy from your pocket and having a game or revealing that you have some of last night's left-over chicken dinner for them to enjoy. The world is a very distracting place for a pup, so it's important to recognize that they're working hard to keep that position by your side.

New Locations

The Service Dog Training Institute[36] suggests that we should build in generalizing training every day. So, with that in mind,

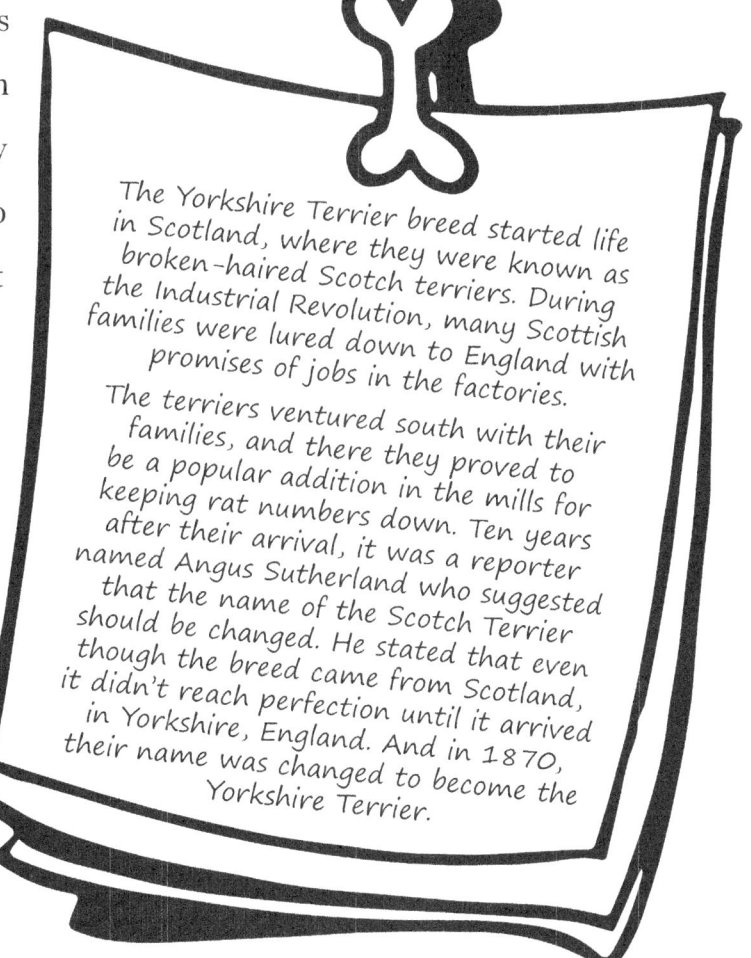

The Yorkshire Terrier breed started life in Scotland, where they were known as broken-haired Scotch terriers. During the Industrial Revolution, many Scottish families were lured down to England with promises of jobs in the factories. The terriers ventured south with their families, and there they proved to be a popular addition in the mills for keeping rat numbers down. Ten years after their arrival, it was a reporter named Angus Sutherland who suggested that the name of the Scotch Terrier should be changed. He stated that even though the breed came from Scotland, it didn't reach perfection until it arrived in Yorkshire, England. And in 1870, their name was changed to become the Yorkshire Terrier.

---

36 https://servicedogtraininginstitute.ca/blog/item/117-generalizing-behaviors-and-tasks-to-many-locations

whenever you need your pup to offer loose leash walking within a new environment, you should begin by making it easier for them to be successful by having a treat in your hand. It won't take them long to realize that it's just the same as other locations and that walking by your side means that good things happen!

Managing Pulling and Distractions

If your pup is pulling even though they were offering you great loose leash walking in the home, that's simply information to tell you that they can't yet cope with that particular environment. Then you have two options:

1. If your Puppy is Completely Overwhelmed

This might happen because the environment is very hectic or busy. It might also be so overwhelming that your puppy just doesn't have the capacity to be able to think about loose leash walking. In this situation, you need to get your pup to a quieter place where they can, once again, focus on you.

Check this out by taking out some treats and asking for some really easy behaviors that they know very well, such as a "sit." Alternatively, you could try and have a game with a favorite toy. If they're not able to take the treat or have a game, then you know that they are still too overwhelmed, and the best option is to head for home.

Don't forget that this is just information, so once you are back home you can think about all the things that your pup found too distracting and then begin training for them. So, if It was in a park and there were lots of children running around, you might want to ask friends with children to come over so that you can practice in the home while the children are playing in the yard.

Sometimes your pup can be overwhelmed because of things that happened before the walk. Perhaps you had very exciting visitors, or your puppy had a fright when a large dog came running over to them. When this is then combined with lots of distractions on the walk, you get what's called trigger stacking. Certified dog trainer Adrienne Farricelli[37] talks about how important it is to understand how cumulative stress can begin to stack up and then affect how your puppy reacts to situations.

2. Your Puppy is Distracted

There is a difference between your pup being overwhelmed and being distracted. When they are distracted, you will still be able to get their attention with food or toys, but it might need more work than normal. In this situation, it's all about making it easier for your puppy to cope with the environment they're in.

Let's say it was the children running around again, but when you moved 50 feet away, your pup could focus on you and offer some lovely loose leash walking. Now you have

---

[37] https://pethelpful.com/dogs/Understanding-Dog-Trigger-Stacking

information on what your puppy's coping distance is – 50 feet. Now you can take a step closer, to 49 feet and have a game, ask for a "sit" and see if your pup is still engaged with you. Slowly you can move closer, all the time checking that your puppy is relaxed and can focus on you.

Congratulations! If you've followed all the steps, you'll now have a pup who thinks that walking by your side is a great place to be. All the treats you've given them during training have built up to create a huge history of reinforcement for being in the right place. When that's combined with ongoing surprise rewards when you're out and about, it'll ensure that you and your pup can look forward to a lifetime of enjoyable walks.

The Labrador has two distinct types: the English and the American. The English Labrador is the type of dog you're likely to see in the show ring. They have a broad head and a much more substantial appearance when compared to the American variety. They also have a thicker coat and shorter legs.

The American Labrador has a much slimmer looking body and has an overall more athletic appearance. Even their tail is thinner! This is a dog that has been bred for their working ability rather than a breed standard.

Behavioral Issues and How to Resolve Them

Sometimes, how we would like our dog to behave can be quite different from how they'd like to. A dog's instincts to chase and hunt, for example, are not what most of us want from our pet dogs. Then we bring them into the home, where we don't want them to express themselves by barking or whining and where there are so many rules about where they may sleep and where they can't. Not to forget that we also decide which food they can have access to and when they eat. Behaviorist John Bradshaw[38] talks about dogs being in crisis, and this is because they have to keep changing the way they live because of the changes happening in our lives.

When you think of it this way, it's not too surprising that so many owners find themselves needing help to live in harmony with their dog. But, with the right knowledge and some planning, you can ensure that your dog's needs are met and that a fantastic relationship begins to grow.

In this chapter, we talk about several issues and how to approach them. Behavior always happens for a reason, and while you could just punish the dog, it doesn't address why the behavior happened to begin with. The dog who destroys the sofa while you're

---

[38] https://www.independent.co.uk/property/house-and-home/pets/features/hounded-out-why-dogs-are-struggling-to-fit-into-modern-life-2307771.html

not there may be suffering immense emotional distress when you leave him alone. So, unless we address those emotions, problems will keep happening. When we truly listen to what our dog is trying to tell us, then we can find ways of living in harmony.

Training a rescue dog

When a rescue dog joins your home, it's such an exciting time for everyone. But you might also be feeling a little nervous about the arrival of your new family member. It will take your dog some time to get used to the routines of their new life and adapt to the new environment, so you do need to be prepared for a settling-in period.

All the techniques explained earlier in the book are also great ways of training your rescue dog. In fact, no matter the age of your rescue dog, treating them as a puppy can be a great way of helping them avoid making mistakes and understand what's needed, right from day one. The Animal Rescue League of Boston[39] also talks about the need for a period of trust-building when your rescue dog first comes home. The "Rule of Three" – three days, three weeks, and three months – helps you to understand how the trust begins to build.

---

39   https://www.arlboston.org/welcoming-your-adopted-dog-into-your-home/

The First Three Days

The first three days are like a "detox period" as your dog transitions from the shelter to your home. For some dogs, it's all overly exciting, and they may find it challenging to settle. For others, it can be overwhelming, and these are the dogs who tend to sleep a lot during those first few days.

It can be a good idea to begin by limiting their access to one area of the home. With all the change going on in their lives, they will be feeling a little stressed, so the smaller the new area they need to cope with, the more comfortable they will be. This also makes it easier for you to watch for signs that they need to toilet and manage any mishaps.

As tempting as it is to provide lots of fuss and attention, hold back to begin with. It'll take a little time to know just where and how your dog likes to be fussed over, so take it slowly and at their pace. The five-second petting rule is an excellent way of asking your dog if they like the way you're petting them. Simply

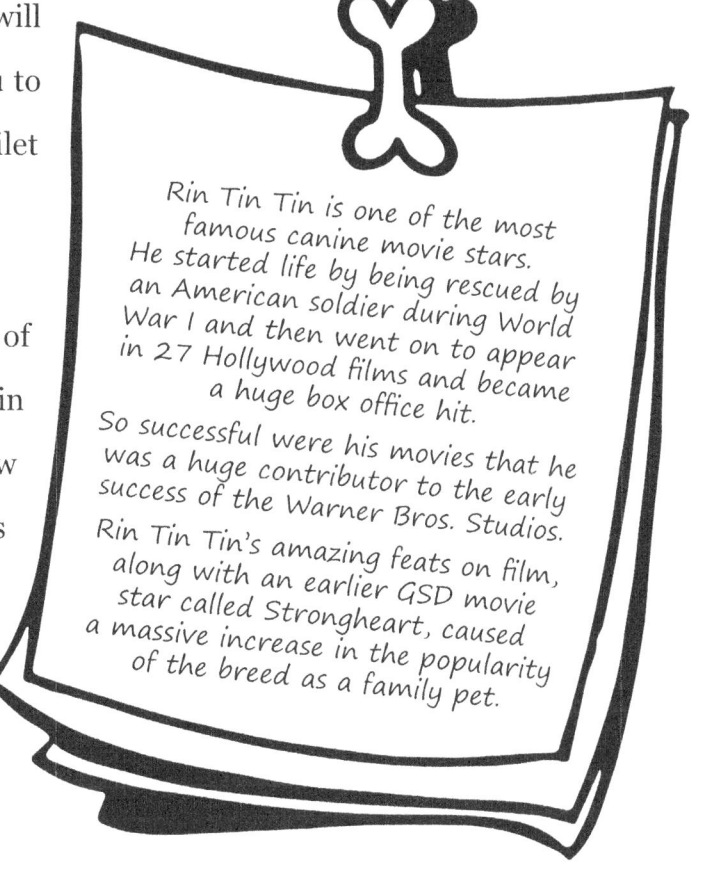

Rin Tin Tin is one of the most famous canine movie stars. He started life by being rescued by an American soldier during World War I and then went on to appear in 27 Hollywood films and became a huge box office hit.
So successful were his movies that he was a huge contributor to the early success of the Warner Bros. Studios.
Rin Tin Tin's amazing feats on film, along with an earlier GSD movie star called Strongheart, caused a massive increase in the popularity of the breed as a family pet.

stroke for five seconds and then stop, if your dog turns away from you, then they've had enough; if they turn towards you, then they would probably like some more.

For some dogs, such as those coming from puppy mills, this might be the very first time they have ever been in a home. So that means that they may not have seen or heard everyday items such as vacuum cleaners and televisions. Try to introduce these slowly and at a distance so that you can check how they react and reassure them if they become worried.

After the First Three Weeks

After three weeks, your dog has become used to your comings and goings, and they know the daily routine for walk and feed times. You'll now also start to see more of their real personality.

You'll find that they are now more relaxed and come to you more readily for fuss and attention. They are also now happy to play with toys, and they have found their favorite places in the home and garden to relax and sleep.

If there have been any behavior problems, you'll soon know if they were a one-off or something for which you may need professional help from a qualified and experienced dog behaviorist.

At this point, the journey is still not without a few bumps, but problems are now likely to be fewer and less stressful.

After the First Three Months

After three months, most dogs now know they are finally home.

You've now visited a number of different locations, met different people, and probably come across a range of different dogs. All of this has helped you to understand how your dog reacts to new situations and experiences.

There will still be some challenges, and there may be times when you might wonder just what you got yourself into. But, with patience and a sense of humor, you will build the foundations on which you can enjoy the journey toward an amazing relationship.

Behavior Problems

If at any point, your dog shows behavior that puts you or your family at risk, you must get in touch with a qualified and experienced canine behaviorist for professional advice.

Aggression

Most aggression is based in fear[40]. So that includes fear of losing a valuable resource such as food or a toy, or fear of being hurt by another dog or a person who is acting in a threatening way. When we think of aggression in this way, it becomes much easier to work out why it's happening and then how to help our dog to cope.

Aggression is the last resort for most dogs; it's a dangerous strategy and one which they avoid unless there is no other choice. This means that there are several different approaches they will try first, and only if not successful will they escalate to the next step. These steps include:

1. Calming signals including turning their head away, yawning and blinking

2. Freezing

3. Growling

4. Snaps

5. Bites

---

40   https://positively.com/dog-behavior/aggression/fear-aggression/

That means that If you see your dog suddenly go very still, that's a warning sign that they are currently feeling threatened by something. If you can remove the threat, then the problem has been avoided, and you can then address helping them to cope with that situation.

If, however, you ignore the freezing, and the environment stays the same, then your dog will have to move to the next stage, to growl. Now you might think of growling as being a bad thing which needs to be punished. But this is just your dog communicating with you that they are feeling pretty concerned about something. If the growl is punished, then your dog must assume that you still don't understand that there is a problem. Now they are forced to take the next step to try and get you to understand what's going on.

This is when you then get an air snap. This, again, is designed to warn you about what's going on. Your dog is very accurate with their teeth, and so if they meant to bite you, it would have happened! Still not listening? Or did you punish the dog? Then here we go again, up to the next stage, this time a bite. Even at this point, many dog bites are relatively minor compared to the damage they could do. If you have ever watched your dog with a bone, then you'll know just how much strength they have and how bad the outcome could be.

But for your dog to get to this stage usually means that they have tried several other ways to tell you they're feeling threatened. Only when you did not respond were they left with no choice but to move to the next option.

You can now see that you never want to punish a growl. You need to ensure that the path of communication is left wide open. When you hear a growl, that's information for you that you need to change something in your dog's environment, and then when everything is calm, either plan how to change the response or call in an expert to help.

Do be aware that medical problems can often be a cause of aggression. One team of researchers found that 50% of dogs[41] who had been involved in a child biting incident had or were suspected of having medical conditions that contributed to the problem. So that means that before starting work on the aggression problems, it's essential for your DOG to have a full veterinary check to rule out any medical issues. Most behaviorists will insist on this happening before they meet your dog.

> Originating from Scotland, the Golden Retriever was developed in the late 1800s by Lord Tweedmouth. He aimed to breed a yellow-colored dog that could retrieve over long distances. He achieved this by crossing a Wavy-Coated Retriever to a Tweed Water Spaniel. Then, over the next 20 years, he strived to perfect his breed by adding in some Red Setter, other retrievers, and it's thought, even a Bloodhound or two.
>
> It was the early 1900s before there was enough consistency in the puppies to be able to register the dogs, which were then known as Golden Flat Coats. Finally, in 1913, they were renamed as the Golden Retriever.

---

41   https://www.ncbi.nlm.nih.gov/pmc/articles/PMC2610618/

Food Related Aggression

Food is a big deal for most dogs. It's the highlight of their day, and when it's been in short supply in the past or taken away, it may become even more valuable.

So, let's imagine our dog, who is feeling a little worried about people being around when he's eating. There are two approaches we can take:

1. Management. This means that our dog always eats in the kitchen by themselves with the door shut. If you live by yourself, this might be a workable solution, but you must remember that you are just managing the situation and not resolving the problem. If you have children or have friends or relatives coming over to stay, then this is a risky strategy. That's because, at some point, someone will forget and walk right in on the dog while they're eating.

2. Change the dog's emotional response to someone being close by when they have food. That means rather than a person being a threat, they now become a predictor of good things happening. To do this:

   a. Provide your dog with their food in the bowl as usual, and then have a supply of good, "much better than what's in your bowl" food.

b. With some of the tasty food in your hand, walk past your dog from a safe distance and toss the food in their direction. Don't stop, don't look at the dog or call their name, simply throw the food, and leave.

c. Repeat over several days until your dog looks up as they hear you coming, and they look excited, interested, and happy to see you.

d. Steadily over several days, come a little closer to your dog, following steps b and c, all the time carefully watching your dog to ensure that they are relaxed with you being there.

e. Repeat a few times every week to keep reminding your dog of how good it is to have people close by when they eat.

The second approach, to change the dog's emotional response, is not about being able to take the food away from your dog. If someone came up to you while you were eating your dinner and took your plate away, the chances are you wouldn't react well. Even if that person is someone that you have great respect for, that you love, or have been friends with for many years. What we want your dog to understand is that if someone should walk past while they have their food, it's no big deal; in fact, it might mean that something really good is heading in their direction!

Many other types of aggression, such as guarding an object, or a bed, can also be resolved in the same way.

While aggression towards people and other dogs can be reduced in intensity, they are very serious issues. There is a significant risk to you, to other people, and your dog's future if it is not managed very carefully. The ASPCA describes aggression cases as being both complex to diagnose and tricky to treat[42]. This means that it's essential to get advice from an experienced professional to safeguard everyone's wellbeing.

Barking

This can be such a frustrating problem behavior and one which can also cause real problems between you and your neighbors. If it's not sorted out quickly, you could find yourself in court and at the receiving end of a hefty fine just like these owners did[43]! So, number one on the list is to work out what's causing the

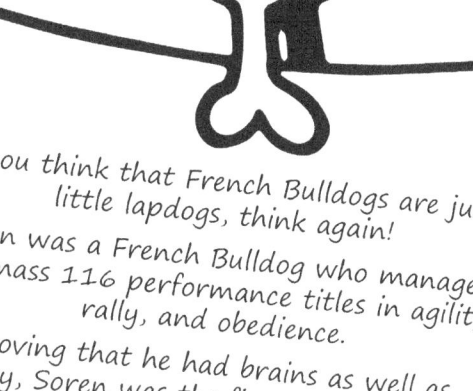

If you think that French Bulldogs are just little lapdogs, think again!

Soren was a French Bulldog who managed to amass 116 performance titles in agility, rally, and obedience.

Proving that he had brains as well as beauty, Soren was the first French Bulldog to earn a Master Agility Championship title from the American Kennel Club!

Soren then became famous through a children's book, "Soaring Soren," which encourages children who face physical or emotional challenges to believe in themselves. Soren's owner, Deborah Stevenson, says that she thinks the secret to Soren's success was simple: "He did what he did because it never occurred to him that he couldn't."

---

42 https://www.aspca.org/pet-care/dog-care/common-dog-behavior-issues/aggression

43 https://www.animallaw.info/topics/barking-dogs?order=title&sort=desc

problem. If you're at home when your dog begins to bark, then it's easy to see what's caused it. It might be someone walking past your home, children playing, or a cat walking through your yard. If the issue happens when you're not there and neighbors are letting you know it's a problem, then that may become a little more complex.

Barking at Something

Let's look at the easy one first, when you're at home, and you can see what's causing the problem. Sometimes these situations are straightforward to resolve; it might be as simple as rearranging the room so that there's no longer a chair in front of the window. Now with no access to look outside, your dog can't see the people walking past to bark at. If the barking is a response to noise, such as another dog barking down the street, then you may find that having background noise, such as the radio or TV on, could be enough to drown out the trigger.

The American Kennel Club[44] suggests that dogs often bark because of boredom and inadequate exercise. And that makes sense – a tired dog is much more likely to sleep and chill out. Along with getting a good walk every day, ideas to relieve boredom include:

 Food puzzle toys

 Training

---
44 https://www.akc.org/expert-advice/training/how-to-stop-dog-barking/

Scent games such as searching for food around the home

 Food stuffed toys

You could also teach your dog a "quiet" cue. To do this, you need some predictability of when your dog will bark. So, if you know the neighbors walk their dog at 8 am, and that causes your dog to bark, then you need to be ready to do some training at that moment. The way to teach the "quiet" command is:

1. Wait for the trigger (the neighbor's dog) to appear.

2. Just before your dog responds, squeak a squeaky toy.

3. As your dog turns to see what's happening, throw some really good treats on the floor.

4. Repeat for several days until you can see your dog looking out of the window and then looking back at you.

5. Then, when your dog spots the neighbors heading in their direction, you can add in the "quiet" cue and reward.

Be careful not to get into what's called a behavior chain, so that when your dog barks, you then say "quiet," and then your dog gets a treat. It's not going to take long for your clever canine to work out how to get more treats!

Barking Because You're Not There

We said that in the second situation, your dog barking when you're not there, may be tougher to resolve. That's because there could be several different things going on. It might be that just as in the first scenario, someone walking past the home or the noise for children playing is what's causing your dog to bark. However, it might also be a separation-related problem. Researchers in the UK have found that up to 50% of all pet dogs show some type of behavior problem when left alone[45]. And this isn't always due to anxiety; it could also happen because of frustration.

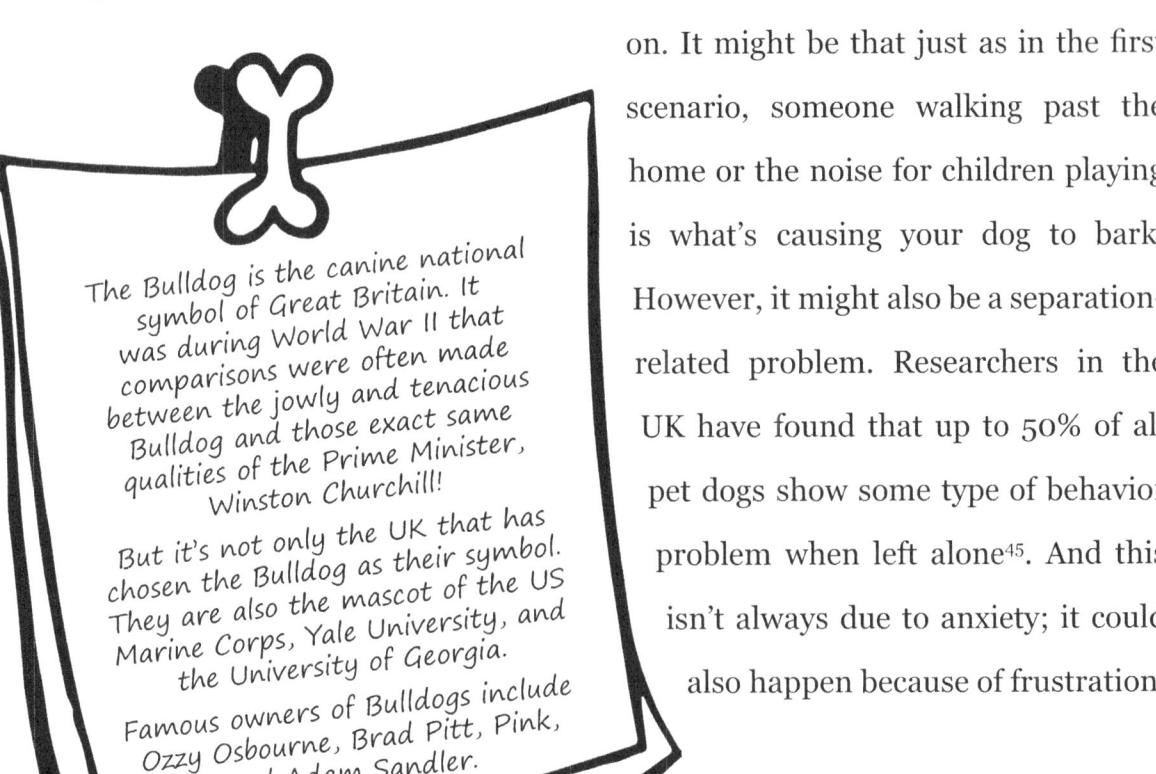

The Bulldog is the canine national symbol of Great Britain. It was during World War II that comparisons were often made between the jowly and tenacious Bulldog and those exact same qualities of the Prime Minister, Winston Churchill!

But it's not only the UK that has chosen the Bulldog as their symbol. They are also the mascot of the US Marine Corps, Yale University, and the University of Georgia.

Famous owners of Bulldogs include Ozzy Osbourne, Brad Pitt, Pink, and Adam Sandler.

---

45   https://www.frontiersin.org/articles/10.3389/fvets.2019.00499/full#h4

The management solution to this problem is for your dog to go to day care as there they will have the company of other dogs and people. However, this does limit when you can go out and not come home to a scene of devastation!

Setting up a remote camera through an app on your phone or leaving a camcorder running can provide you with lots of information on what's going on in your absence. You may then see that your dog only barks when someone walks past the window, in which case leaving your dog in a different room may resolve the problem. But you may also see your dog becoming very distressed as you leave home, and that then results in a barking response.

In most cases, this will need you to book time off work to be able to implement a behavior modification plan provided by a behaviorist. This will require you to slowly build up the time that your dog can be left, but it will be essential that at no time during the process is your dog left for longer than they can cope with.

Now, this is a problem that can be successfully resolved, but it takes time and real commitment to get there. However, when your dog is calm and confident about being left alone, they'll be less likely to bark and to destroy your belongings!

Chewing

When we talk about inappropriate chewing, we have to consider: inappropriate to who?

For your puppy, it's not inappropriate in the slightest; you, however, may have a different opinion when you spot the trail of destruction!

Puppies need to chew. Between the ages of around three and seven months, puppies are teething, and chewing helps them to relieve the discomfort they're feeling. Chewing is also a biological need as it also helps to move on the puppy teeth and allow the adult teeth to come through the gums. Our puppies are also great explorers, and they do that by picking things up in their mouths.

Avoiding the Problem to Begin With

The first step is to consider how easy you're making it for your puppy to avoid getting into trouble. Take a wander around the rooms where your pup lives and look for anything which might be too tempting. TV remotes, for example, seem to be irresistible, so make sure they have a safe place well above your pup's reach. Remember, this isn't forever; this is just the same as keeping valuable or dangerous items away from toddlers.

Then think about how you're going to keep your pup and your possessions safe when you're not around to supervise. You might have a room where there is little which can be chewed, or you may decide on a crate. Do remember that crates should only be used for short periods and that your pup needs to be gradually introduced to them to ensure they're relaxed and happy to be in them.

Providing Good Alternatives

The next step is to think about what your pup can have to chew. Some dog toys are pretty dull, so we need ones that your pup is going to love, and which can stand up to those sharp little puppy teeth!

Thinking about those aching gums, toys that have been in the freezer can be really soothing. Just pop the toy into a bag and then into the freezer, then it's all ready to go when needed.

There is now a fantastic range of toys that can be stuffed with food. Fill them lightly, to begin with, and until your pup works out how to get at all the goodies. Then you can increase the challenge by really compacting

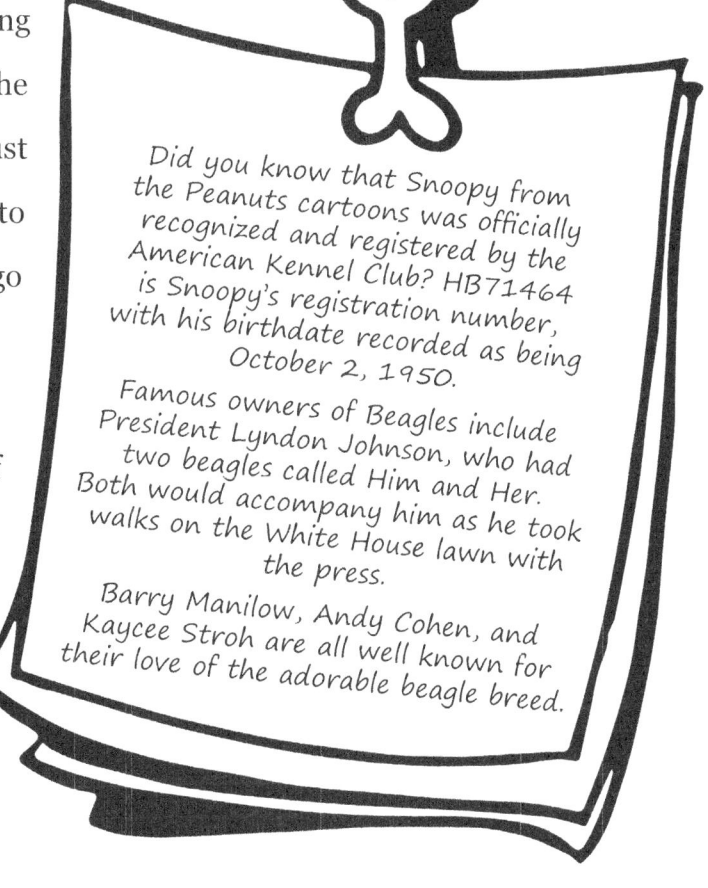

Did you know that Snoopy from the Peanuts cartoons was officially recognized and registered by the American Kennel Club? HB71464 is Snoopy's registration number, with his birthdate recorded as being October 2, 1950.

Famous owners of Beagles include President Lyndon Johnson, who had two beagles called Him and Her. Both would accompany him as he took walks on the White House lawn with the press.

Barry Manilow, Andy Cohen, and Kaycee Stroh are all well known for their love of the adorable beagle breed.

the food inside and by popping them into the freezer once stuffed. Keep a few ready to go for when you need your pup to be kept busy.

You'll also find all kinds of chews in the local pet store. Make sure they're suitable for a pup before buying, and we'd recommend supervising chewing to begin with, until you know they're safe for your youngster.

When Things Go Wrong

So, what should you do if your pup does chew on something they shouldn't? Well, grab a newspaper, roll it up, and then whack yourself over the head! Because puppies need supervision, or they need to be in an environment where they can't get into trouble, and that's our responsibility. In all seriousness, it's essential to shift the blame away from the pup. Simply move them from whatever they're chewing and find them a better alternative. Then work out how you can avoid that situation happening again.

Puppy chewing doesn't last forever, so supply lots of great options for your youngster, and you will soon see them growing up into a great family dog.

Adult Dogs Chewing

If your older dog begins chewing things they shouldn't, then a visit to the vet is first on the list. Toothache or gum infections could be the reason why the chewing has begun, and once that's sorted out, you may find the problem disappears.

If you've taken on an older rescue dog, it may be that they've never been in a house before, or that they've never had the freedom to wander around. This means they've never had the opportunity to learn what is allowed and what isn't. In this situation, the best approach is to provide them with the opportunity to learn the things they missed out on by following all the advice given for a pup.

Jumping up

New people are exciting, and people coming home is just the best! Pups seem to jump up at us instinctively, and one school of thought is that they do this because when they greet another dog, they do it nose to nose[46]. So, jumping up at us allows them to say hello in precisely the same way.

Now, we said that jumping up seems to be instinctive, but you should know that we humans are also pretty awful at encouraging something which we then decide we

---

[46] https://www.psychologytoday.com/gb/blog/canine-corner/201510/nose-nose-greeting-puppies

don't want our dogs to do anymore. When we see that cute little puppy, and we tap our legs to encourage them to run over, and then we fuss over them when they jump up? Well, we have just helped that behavior to continue even when they're a 30kg adult dog! And when we come home in our gym kit, or we're in relaxed weekend clothes, we let our dogs jump up. That's pretty confusing for our puppy when we then tell them off for jumping up when we're all dressed up to go out or when we've returned home from the office in work clothes.

The first thing to decide are the house rules that "everyone" follows; the more consistent you are, the easier it becomes for your puppy to be right. Maybe they can jump up when you tell them they can; you could use a word like "up" to let them know that it's okay. Or you may decide that you never want that to happen. Now, everyone makes mistakes, including your dog, so while we can't say they will never jump up again, we can increase the likelihood of them keeping four paws on the floor using one of the following methods.

> You might associate Poodles with France, but the background of the breed is a hotly debated subject amongst their fans.
>
> That's because some believe that they were developed in Germany as a duck retrieving water dog. However, others are of the opinion that they originated in France and are descendants of the French water dog, the Barbet.

How to Stop Biting

Puppy Biting

Puppies come with razor-sharp teeth, and they can hurt! But our pups explore the world with their teeth, so it's not too surprising that they also investigate us in the same way. There is an upside to this, though, as you now have the perfect opportunity to teach your puppy how to be incredibly careful with human skin. Some pups are naturally very soft-mouthed, while others may need your help to learn this skill.

Gentle games to encourage your puppy to control their bite will help you to get great results. We've provided details of two games that are fun for your pup and will encourage quick learning.

Game 1 - To Get the Treat, You Need to Leave the Treat Alone

Having a treat in your hand can cause your pup to nibble and bite to get at it as soon as possible. This game trains your dog that they can always have the treat but only by being polite.

1. Place a treat in your hand and wrap your fingers around it tightly.

2. Now offer your hand to your pup.

3. No matter how much they try to get it, your hand doesn't open.

4. The moment they stop trying to get it your hand opens, and they can have the treat.

Your timing is critical here; you're just looking for your pup's nose to come away from your hand for a moment before opening it to give them access to the treat.

Avoid saying anything; you're not telling your dog to leave it. Instead, they are learning through the consequences of their behavior.

Game 2 - Swaps!

Your puppy must learn to stop biting if a game becomes too rough. This game teaches your puppy to remove something from their mouth when asked. That could be anything, from tugging on the sleeve of your jumper to something they have taken, which may be dangerous for them to have.

For this game, you need a toy that your pup enjoys playing with and some tasty treats.

1. Get your pup really involved in a game with you so that you're playing tug (but do be careful of puppy teeth – just tug very gently!).

2. While you're still playing, bring a treat right up to your pup's nose.

3. The moment they let go of the toy, give them the treat. If your pup doesn't let go, try the game again, but this time with a less exciting toy.

4. When your pup reliably lets go when they see the treat, you can then use a word to let them know what they need to do, which might be something like "out" or "leave."

5. Now your pup will let go of their favorite toy because they know there's a great alternative!

The next stage is to generalize the behavior. By this, we mean that your pup can not only let go of their favorite toy, but they will also let go of any toy or item when asked.

Yorkies are well known for their beautifully flowing, long coats. But new owners should be aware that this stunning feature is also crazily time-consuming to take care of. That's because the Yorkies coat is very similar to human hair, which means that it quickly tangles into knots if it's not brushed every single day.
Many pet owners have their Yorkshire Terriers trimmed into a "puppy cut" which makes it much easy to manage and still looks very cute.

1. Gather together some of your pup's other toys and other household items which are non-dangerous but which they may find attractive. Think about things like socks and gloves.

2. Play the game in a small room where you can shut the door; you don't want your pup to disappear into the yard with your sock!

3. Now select each item, let your pup sniff it and take it into their mouth, and then ask them to leave it and reward with a treat.

4. If your pup isn't very food motivated and would rather play with a toy instead, that's fine; you can use the opportunity to play with their favorite toy instead.

Remember throughout this training that the word you're using is a request rather than a threat. The aim is for your dog to remove something from their mouth happily and willingly.

Final words

Hi again,

And thanks for reading! I bet you still have questions, but I humbly hope there are fewer of those than at the beginning.

That's important to me, since the reason I became a self-published author was to provide young puppy parents like you with ideas they really need and to address their real pain.

So please let me know how I'm doing in this way – by simply leaving a comment on the Amazon book page. And please share your thoughts on the further topics you want me to explore and cover – I will read and respond to all the comments I get.

Thank you so much for your attention and participation.

Sincerely yours,
Wendy

Made in the USA
Coppell, TX
29 December 2020